"*The Kiss* is a darkly beautiful book, fearless and frightening, ironic and compassionate. This is a writer at the top of her form, entirely the master of her material."
—Mary Gordon, author of *The Shadow Man*

In this extraordinary memoir, one of today's best young American writers transforms into a work of art the darkest passage imaginable in a young woman's life: an obsessive love affair between father and daughter that began when the author, then twenty years old, was reunited with the father whose absence had haunted her youth. Exquisitely and hypnotically written, like a bold and terrifying dream, *The Kiss* is breathtaking in its honesty, power, and beauty. It is a story about taboo, about family complicity in breaking taboo, and about the most primal of love triangles: the one that ensnares a child between mother and father.

"Harrison's story is her own, but is is also a brilliant fiction, densely mythic, sometimes almost liturgical sounding and raw. She is both author and protagonist of a dark pilgrim's progress...Her true fellow travelers are not Oprah and Ricki but Faulkner and Emily Dickinson."
—*Atlanta Journal and Constitution*

"A haunting journey not easily forgotten."
—*People*

"Harrison implicates us in grisly truths we don't want to know (but we do, we do): How rage can parade as love; how heartbreakingly hopeless, yet entirely inevitable, are all attempts to transcend loss; how deep sorrow so often transmogrifies into deep viciousness, instead of deep compassion; how those who are most damaged by their parents are the least able to walk—or even crawl—away from them...Like all good literature, *The Kiss* illuminates something that we knew already, while also teaching us things we had not even suspected."
—*Los Angeles Times*

Also by Kathryn Harrison

EXPOSURE
POISON
THICKER THAN WATER

The Kiss

The Kiss

KATHRYN HARRISON

AN AVON BOOK

Kathryn Harrison is the author's married name. She has not used her maiden name in a number of years.

A portion of this work, entitled "Seeking Rapture: Lessons for an Apprentice Saint," appeared in the September 1994 issue of *Harper's*.

AVON BOOKS, INC.
1350 Avenue of the Americas
New York, New York 10019

Front cover photograph by Joyce Ravid
Published by arrangement with Random House, Inc.
Visit our website at **http://www.AvonBooks.com/Bard**
ISBN: 0-380-73147-9

First Bard Printing: June 1998

Printed in the U.S.A.

OPM 10 9 8 7 6 5 4 3 2 1

Beloved

1942–1985

We are, all of us, molded and remolded by those who have loved us, and though that love may pass, we remain none the less *their* work—a work that very likely they do not recognize, and which is never exactly what they intended.

—François Mauriac, *The Desert of Love*

The Kiss

We meet at airports. We meet in cities where we've never been before. We meet where no one will recognize us.

One of us flies, the other brings a car, and in it we set out for some destination. Increasingly, the places we go are unreal places: the Petrified Forest, Monument Valley, the Grand Canyon—places as stark and beautiful and deadly as those revealed in satellite photographs of distant planets. Airless, burning, inhuman.

Against such backdrops, my father takes my face in his hands. He tips it up and kisses my closed eyes, my throat. I feel his fingers in the hair at the nape of my neck. I feel his hot breath on my eyelids.

We quarrel sometimes, and sometimes we weep. The road always stretches endlessly ahead and behind us, so that we are out of time as well as out of place. We go to Muir Woods in northern California, so shrouded in blue fog that the road is lost; and we drive down the Natchez Trace into deep, green Mississippi summer. The trees bear blossoms as big as my head; their ivory petals drift to the ground and cover our tracks.

Separated from family and from the flow of time, from work and from school; standing against a sheer face of red rock one thousand feet high; kneeling in a cave dwelling two thousand years old; watching as a million bats stream from the mouth of Carlsbad Caverns into the purple dusk—these nowheres and no-times are the only home we have.

My mother's parents raise me. I live in their house until I'm seventeen. In it, my father's name is never spoken, his existence is not acknowledged.

"Where's your dad?" other children ask. "I don't know," I answer.

"Why?" they ask, but I don't know what to say to that either.

He and my mother divorce when I am six months old. I stay with her and her parents; he leaves.

My father is an absence, a hole like one of those my grandmother cuts out of family photographs. Rather than discard the entire picture of an event that includes someone she dislikes, she snips the offender out with untidy haste, using her manicure scissors.

I sit on the foot of her bed and watch her edit the family albums, a task she undertakes with the kind of grim determination that can only have been inspired by a fight with my mother. Often, she cuts out only the heads and leaves the anonymous bodies behind as a reminder of her displeasure, and her ruthlessness. No one is safe from her censorship; from the albums she excises unflattering images of herself as well.

The few snapshots my mother has of my father she keeps hidden. If I ask to look at one, she might show it to me. In every photograph, he is a tiny figure in a suit and glasses; the only person in the frame, still, he is never in its center or its foreground, he seems as incidental as a bystander. I can't make out his features.

The closed door to my grandparents' bedroom is visible from the entrance to our house. When a young man arrives to pick my mother up for a date, when my grandmother hears my mother greet him and go to get her coat, she begins to scream from behind her closed bedroom door. My grandmother has a talent for screaming. Her screams are not human. They tear through the veil of ordinary life—the life that moments before surrounded the unsuspecting young man in the foyer—and in rushes every black, bleak, and barbarous thing: animals with legs caught in traps, surgery in the days that precede anesthesia, the shriek of a scalded infant, the cry of a young woman raped in the woods, the long howl of the werewolf who catches her scent, who finds and devours what's left of her.

I am four, and when I hear my grandmother scream I fall to my knees and crawl to safety, either under a table or, if I can get that far, into the linen closet or the wood bin.

My mother sleeps. For as long as she lives with us, in her parents' house, she sleeps whenever she can. She sleeps very late every day, as much as six or seven hours past the time when I get up for breakfast. I stand beside her bed as she sleeps.

Wake up. Wake up. I think the thought so loudly inside my head that it seems as if she will have to rise, she can't remain insensible to my imploring her—my wanting her—as fervently as I do. I never understand that she has fled into sleep, that she seeks comfort in sleep, that sleep is where she hides. I know only that I can't bear to let her do it.

Her eyes closed and hidden behind her satin sleep mask, her face as flat and white as the mask is flat and black: this terrifies me. Sleep makes my mother's face itself into a mask, one mask under another. She draws each breath so shallowly it seems as if she must be dying, that she might never wake.

I go into her bathroom and run the water from the taps. I flush the toilet, pick up her hairbrush and set it down hard on the counter, drop a shoe, close a door. I make any noise I can that might rouse my mother but that can't be judged as a direct and purposeful assault on the fortress of her sleeping. Because for as long as my mother refuses consciousness, she refuses consciousness of me: I do not exist. As I stand watching her sleep I feel the world open behind me like a chasm. I know I can't step even an inch back from her bed without plummeting.

If I dare, I reach forward and gently touch the smooth sheen of her black mask. It looks illicit, almost perverse, bordered by a narrow ruffle of black lace, the kind I already associate with the underwear she puts on before a date. Outside, I hear birds, awake as I have been for hours; their calls sound shrill and pitiless.

If I wake her, she doesn't talk to me. She stalks around her room as if enraged, a wild and astonished look on her face. I make myself small; I back into the corner by the door, and often she doesn't seem to know I'm there. She takes a cigarette from the pack left on her writing desk, and then she stands before the French doors that lead from her bedroom to the garden. As she smokes, she stares out, her back toward me, and the light comes through the glass and outlines her body under the thin white gown. Smoke rises from her mouth, her hand. It rises slowly, dizzily, swaying back and forth like a snake charmer's flute.

Her eyes, when they turn at last toward me, are like two empty mirrors. I can't find myself in them.

Though she dates other men and even accepts their engagement rings, my mother remains romantically fixated, albeit mostly from a distance, on my father. Her gaze is so firmly held by this absent, invisible man, that as a child I think I see him in my grandparents' house. Having looked carefully at those tiny images in a dark suit, I see a specter of a similar man, usually at dusk, standing among the living-room's shadows, or slipping down the hall to the bedrooms.

"What does he look like?" asks a friend of the family, a woman afflicted with fits of clairvoyance, and whose eyeglasses swing out on a necklace of blue glass beads when she bends down to talk to me. "Tell me," she says, compelled by my grandmother's report that I've seen a ghost in our house.

"He doesn't have a face," I whisper.

"Guardian angel!" she cries.

"In a suit?" says my grandmother. "Surely angels don't wear suits!"

The ghost frightens me. He doesn't speak or gesture. He never follows when I run from the dark rooms in which I think I see him. But he provokes me in his silence, the way he seems, without eyes, to stare. I grow afraid of the dark, and at bedtime I require night-lights, Ovaltine, my grandfather's singing over and over the talismanic "K-K-K-Katie," and a magic row of eleven stuffed bears set along the wall by my bed. Still, I wake screaming.

Perhaps my father really is there in spirit: standing in our house, waiting, pacing among tables and chairs in the living room we never use. For me he is. As his second wife will tell me years later, she takes as her husband a man who is not entirely present to her, who is always looking back over his shoulder at my mother and at me.

"When I married your father," she will say, "I knew

he would always be in love with her. I knew that your mother was a part of him, inseparable from the person I fell in love with."

A "man of God" is how someone describes my father to me. I don't remember who. Not my mother. I'm young enough that I take the words to mean he has magical properties and that he is good, better than other people.

He sends long letters to my mother, and sometimes, folded in with them, are little ones for me. In them, my father describes his work as a minister. He takes Christian youth groups into the slums, where they rebuild people's homes. They paint the walls white and bring blankets, food, and toys for children who have no toys. I have everything a child could possibly want, my father tells me. He hopes I'll have the opportunity to experience some poor people, because otherwise how will I learn to be grateful?

A letter dated two days after my fifth birthday inquires if I had fun. Did I have a party? On that day, my father was in a home where people don't have money to celebrate birthdays. He met a child there, a little boy who looked like an angel and who was very smart but had crossed eyes. My father is seeing what he can do to have his vision corrected.

Ashamed that I don't persevere bravely in a slum, and ashamed of my clear vision, I begin to cross my eyes experimentally.

"They'll get stuck like that if you don't stop," my grandmother warns, and she tells me that if the direction of the wind changes while I do it, they'll remain crossed forever, I might as well be blind.

At Thanksgiving, my mother arranges for an edifying way for the two of us to celebrate the holiday. From a social service agency she gets the name of a needy family who is willing for us to come and prepare dinner for them. In the home we visit, several children share a room half the size of mine at my grandparents'. When I add flour to the gravy too quickly and pour nutmeg on the floor, my mother isn't angry as she would be at home. She doesn't yell or snatch anything out of my hands.

The meal we cook is consumed in silence. The children eat quickly and furtively; my throat constricts, knowing as I do that the visit has been prompted not by generosity, but by my father's desire that I have an appreciation of what it is I have to be thankful for.

I don't remember writing to my father, but I must have, because after my mother dies I'll find letters from him among her papers, and in them observations about how well I am learning to print and to spell. One faded, penciled note, dated February 20 of the year I turned three, thanks her for sending a Valentine inscribed to "Daddy." *I've never known whether our daughter knows anything of me,* he writes. *Does she? Would it be possible for me to see her for a few hours?*

I'm six when my mother moves out and leaves me. She is gone, but her room remains just as it was. I pull down the coverlet and see that fresh sheets are on her bed, and in her closet hang the dresses she didn't like well enough to take with her. Dresses of all colors: red, blue, pink, green. I stand among them. I duck under the skirt of one and let it fall around me like a yellow tent, a tent the color of the sun and smelling of flowers. I push my face into the smooth fabric, a hundred times more lovely than any other thing in this house. If a dress like this was not worth taking, how could I have hoped to be?

I look in the drawers and see where she keeps her spare nightgown, and I lie carefully on her bed with my head on her pillow. When I get up, I smooth the covers back in place. I make sure that if she returns, she won't know I've been there.

She's moved to a nearby apartment, although to protect herself from my predatory grandmother she never tells us what street she lives on, nor does she give us her phone number. She sees me often, but she comes and goes at her own discretion: she does not want to be summoned by fevers or nightmares or lost teeth. It's the first of my mother's attempts since the divorce to make an independent life for herself, a life that does not seem possible to her unless motherhood is left behind.

My father and I don't exchange letters again until I'm a freshman in college and have, for the first time in my life, an address separate from that of the rest of my family. At school, there's no one other than the postmaster to witness who might send me mail, or how often.

The letters my father writes me are stiff, formal, unimaginative. They betray little of the man himself, but propound tedious theories of education and aesthetics. As with the letters he sent when I was small, their purpose is to instruct. When I read them, standing in the drafty corridor outside my post-office box, I am consumed by frustration. Can anyone really talk and think this way? Is he erudite, or is he what my grandmother would call a "crashing bore"?

Following my father's example, I write careful, pinched responses that require drafts and redrafts, the final copies folded carefully in thirds and sealed in spotless white envelopes.

My mother and father met in the lobby of a theater, where they were introduced to each other by a mutual friend. They were seventeen, and both virgins. Knowing this about my parents is powerful enough to make seventeen the age at which I, too, lose my virginity. I cast it off as if that birthday ordains my doing so; and my partner is also a boy whose inexperience equals mine.

What followed the night of the play, the night my parents met, was not unusual: infatuation, feverish meetings, pregnancy, a hasty marriage, the birth of a child, and then divorce—all of which was played out in my mother's parents' home, as my father's family lived far away from the boarding school he attended. My parents became parents while still children, without money, with no more than high school educations.

"She enjoys reading and attending concerts, and hopes someday to become a dramatic actress," reads the legend below my mother's yearbook picture.

Years after her death, I cut her page from the book's binding. I keep it framed in my study, and sometimes I take it and hold it in my hands. I look carefully at the photograph and at the words I know by heart.

How solemn she is, how unnervingly still for a girl of eighteen, and how much care she has taken with her clothes and her hair, the perfectly plucked brows over her wide hazel eyes. They are dangerous, those eyes in the picture, unplumbed pools of sorrow into which I can tumble and drown. My mother's expression is one that betrays the kind of fear and vulnerability I associate with orphans or refugees, people who have lost everything. Her mouth is small, precise, virginal, her lips closed against appetite. The Cupid's bow of her upper lip is drawn with an exactitude that makes my own look comparatively blurred, unfocused.

Do I know my mother any better than the long-ago classmate, "J.M.," who foretold her future? "She will study literature, French and drama," J.M. wrote. This all comes true, incidentally, although my mother pursues these interests on her own, she doesn't ever go to college.

As for my father, suddenly faced with unimaginable responsibilities—"How will you support them!" I'm told my grandfather cried. "How can you possibly!"—he takes a job as an encyclopedia salesman.

My grandparents' library includes a set of dark-red *Britannicas*. They're on the highest shelf, so I have to stand on a chair to reach them, their tops furred with dust. The binding of the first of the supplementary yearbooks is stamped *1962,* the year after that of my birth.

How many times during my childhood do I take down one of those heavy volumes, use it for a school project or just to satisfy my own curiosity? How many times do I hold one of those books in my arms not knowing who sold them to my grandparents? Cotton gin. Gregor Mendel. The major exports of China. The pollen dance of bees.

My mother and my grandmother speak French fluently, my mother with an accent so flawless that even Parisians comment upon it. "Not possible," they say. "You must have lived in France as a child." As for me, despite lessons begun at age two, for years I make no progress beyond *la table, le crayon,* words that are the same as those in English. Intelligence tests confirm my mother's suspicion that my failure is due to stubbornness rather than lack of aptitude, and she sets out to break me. Willing or not, I am to be ushered into this language of conflict, the one in which my mother and grandmother fight, and which when allied they use to secretly eviscerate their foes.

Each weekend, my mother drills me with flash cards. She bribes, threatens, cajoles. Nothing works. At the shortest Gallic syllable I retreat, not purposefully but helplessly, into a place deep within myself—one from which I can hear her only distantly, as if she is calling down into a well, but cannot respond. Anger, my mother's in particular, renders me almost mute from the time I am small; and my silence always tends to enrage her. Once, she throws the flash cards down and slaps my face.

In the second grade, after five years of failure, I prepare for a French test in a way I have never done before. We have been told to memorize the colors. Red = *Rouge.* Yellow = *Jaune.* Green = *Vert.* I write all the equivalents on a slip of paper and hide it in my sleeve. The test is a mimeographed picture of a clown holding a bunch of balloons, and on each balloon is the

French word for one of the colors. With our crayons we are to color them in appropriately.

My mother's excitement over my perfect score is devastating. She hugs me, she kisses me, she buys me gifts; and even at the age of seven I understand how damning is my success—that my mother's love for me (like her mother's for her) depends on my capitulation. She will accept, acknowledge, *see* me only in as much as I will make myself the child who pleases her.

"I knew you could! I knew you could, if only you tried!" she says. I pull out of her arms, sobbing.

"I can't!" I cry. "I did it with this!" I shove the grubby crib note at her.

"You— You—" My mother splutters, so livid that she can't speak in any language.

The next day she takes me to the teacher, and with her hand tight around the back of my neck I confess. Then she drives me home to my grandparents'. In the driveway, she reaches across my chest to open the passenger door. "Get out," she says. I do, and she leaves.

That night, I come down with an illness no one can define or cure. It begins like the stomach flu but doesn't stop. It goes on for weeks, until the day I overhear the pediatrician tell my grandmother that I'm so dehydrated I'll have to be hospitalized, and then it does stop, as suddenly as it began.

I return to school not just thinner but seemingly smaller than I was before I left, pale, and with my hair cut very short to keep it clean while I was sick.

"Why, this isn't the same child!" the teacher exclaims, as does the principal and everyone who sees me.

"She's a different child! Who is this child!" I hear it ten or more times.

And I am different. I learn French, never with the ease of other subjects and never with pleasure, but I learn it well enough so that I can still read a French novel. Very occasionally, I dream in French, and on those mornings I wake up ill: I vomit.

Do my father's accomplishments cost him as dearly as mine do me? He is one of those men who rises far enough from his roots that among old acquaintances he is held exemplary, and probably in turn despised. How many of his old friends and family—the community from whom success makes him an exile—see what I will discover: that rage has been what motivated him?

. . .

It was in the garden, between the rose bed and the fruit trees, that my grandfather told my father that it was over between him and my mother—my father could forget about calling her his wife. The bargain was simple. If my father would leave without causing the family further trouble, then he could consider himself free: the divorce settlement would require nothing of him.

My grandfather made it clear that there was nothing anyone wanted from him. Not child support; not visits, either.

My grandparents thought they could end it, erase my mother's unfortunate mistake. There was the baby, of course, the life that sprang from my mother's rebellion, her attempt to thwart her parents and especially her mother's desire to control her—there was me to consider, but I was a cost they'd accept. He, however, had to go.

Worn down by her mother's campaign to oust her husband, one which, cannily, focused on the very extravagance my mother's upbringing encouraged, my mother succumbed to the fear that with my father she would always be poor. *Poor* is something that my grandmother, herself raised by a father with a fortune, can make seem very desperate, even fatal.

A preacher's wife! I can hear the disdain with which my grandmother uttered the words.

The earliest directive either I or my mother received from her Jewish parents was to form ourselves in opposition to the children around us. Born in London, my grandmother and grandfather have lived all over the world. They've always considered America a land of convenience, hygiene, and safety, and one in which children are "dragged," as opposed to "brought," up. What an inspired flight of defiance was my mother's choice of my father: his German immigrant ancestors, the miscegenation of his Native American grandmother, not one but two missionary grandfathers, his own parents' broken marriage, not to mention their relatively modest circumstances. How irresistible he must have been to my mother, and how appalling to her parents.

My father, with his tenuous origins, found my grandparents awesome in their entitled European condescension, their wealth and property and the solid history implied by antiques that were passed down, not acquired. If my grandparents still frighten me, raised as I was to assume their mantle of entitlement, how much more they must have frightened my father at nineteen, far from home, the money for his senior year at a fancy prep school scratched together as a kind of apology from his father.

My father's father was a philanderer. As my father tells me years later, he often left his wife and children to pursue other women. The finishing touch to my father's high school career—a diploma from a name-brand prep school and thus a chance at a better college—was intended as a kind of compensation for earlier neglect. In that it gave my father the opportunity to meet my mother, it did change his life. But not in the ways his father must have hoped.

Twenty years old. My life is that of a fugitive. I'm always in an airline terminal, trudging after him over expanses of stained carpet and dull linoleum. The walls around us warn of illegal transport. Arrows point to baggage claims and taxi stands. Everywhere there are small blue signs bearing international symbols for food, first aid, toilets.

Our protracted good-byes are consumed along

with magazines and junk food by the weary, bored travelers who surround us, slumped in molded plastic chairs.

Do we resemble each other enough that people suspect we're father and daughter? Do we sit too close to one another? Does his hand on my arm betray his intent? And why do we cling so, as if our parting will be as final as death?

People fix their eyes on us without embarrassment, as unabashed in their staring as if our movements and speech issue from one of the coin-op televisions in the waiting area.

Sometimes, in the airport stores, my father buys greeting cards, big ones with roses and lace and matching pink envelopes. I watch as he writes in them, stamps and mails them, too, so that our visit will not interrupt their relentless flow to my address.

As I grow up, I know little of my father's life: He has a new wife and another daughter. It snows where he lives. He has hay fever and a large dog called a malamute that once ate a cat. He's a doctor, but not the medical kind—he has something called a PhD. My source of such details is my mother, because the infrequent letters stop, and there are only two visits during which I can observe him myself.

He arrives the summer I am five, and my mother, my father, and I go to the beach together. My father wears a long-sleeved shirt and canvas shoes into the surf. He walks out until a wave breaks over his shoulders, and then he turns back. I watch him make his way up the sand to our umbrella. The shoes squelch and the shirt's tails and cuffs drip. He sits in one of our folding chairs, and water streams in rivulets down its aluminum legs. He spreads a towel over his white knees. What frightens me most about him is the way he fascinates my mother. I am sure, watching as they pack up the beach equipment and walk toward the car, that if I didn't follow, they wouldn't notice I was missing.

He brings a large camera with him, and one afternoon he poses me before it. In the photographs he takes I'm wearing a yellow dress with tight elastic at the waist and sleeves, and I remember that dress, how uncomfortably it gripped the top of my arms. In memory its hold is not distinguishable from that of his large-fingered hand as he guides me into the positions he wants.

When he returns, I'm ten, and the three of us go to the art museum and to the farmers' market. At the museum, my mother and father hold hands and I trail several yards behind, all of us perspiring and moving with dull languor through the airless galleries. At one point, I put my hot hands on the cool foot of a huge marble statue of Venus, and my father wheels around and reprimands me. "Hasn't anyone taught you not to touch things in a museum!" he says, and he looks disapprovingly at both my mother and me.

At lunch in the farmers' market my chair is pushed uncomfortably close to the table's edge, so close that I feel I can't breathe, and I am on the floor a good deal of the time, retrieving silverware I've nervously dropped. I sense that my father regards me with some curiosity—his child, after all—and little pleasure. I am, as I have been from my birth, the inevitable compromise of my parents' privacy.

Ten years later—ten years after the day I look at his black shoes from my vantage under the table—everything has changed. My father mails me cassette tapes he's made, and I play them on my car's tape deck. I drive to a shopping center a few miles from the university's post office, and with the car doors locked, I use my thumbnail to slit the tape sealing the small white box.

His voice fills the car. It rises, falls, begs, breaks. *Girl,* he calls me. *Oh, girl. My girl.* Alone in my car, I put my hands over my face as I listen. I am no less enslaved to him than I have been to my mother.

I play the tape over and over, pushing the rewind button so that I can hear as often as I like the sound of my father telling me he wants me.

His recorded voice is something I will keep forever, and something that, when it's over, I won't allow myself to hear. Like his letters and photographs, the cassettes will be locked in a trunk, returning him—all evidence of the man—to his original relationship to me: the lost father.

I tell my mother that I want to send my father a gift, something I make myself. It must be that I hope to erase or at least mitigate the poor impression I'm afraid I made on him during the last visit, when he scolded me in the sculpture gallery.

"What about one of your paintings?" she suggests.

I'm enrolled in an art class that meets on Wednesdays after school.

"All right," I agree.

In the class, I'm learning to paint in oils the traditional way, by copying existing works, often reproductions featured on calendars or torn from old greeting cards. The one I use as a model for my father's painting is of a red barn surrounded by yellow fields and haystacks. I choose it because, sitting across the table in the farmers' market, my father told me that he drives past farms while traveling between the two small churches he serves.

The barn's door is open and no interior shows, only a black shadow. I sketch the picture's outlines onto my canvas with a pencil, and over the next weeks I paint the yellow hay and the barn's red roof and sides. The trotting-horse weather vane, which I expect to be so difficult, turns out nicely, and it's the seemingly simple part that goes awry. I can't paint the black rectangle of shadow formed by the open barn door so that it looks even; it's wobbly on both sides.

I set out to make the shadow right. I work on the doorway for months, trying to get it perfect. At one point, the teacher tries to take the canvas away, but I won't let her, and week by week the shadow grows bigger and bigger, its outlines no less uneven. Masking tape and a straight edge don't help. When I at last give up, I see that in the effort to perfect the shadow, I've made it so big that the doorway almost fills the outlines of the barn itself. As I sat before my easel, I fell headlong into a dark square of uncertainty, whose limits I tried over and over to define, never getting them right.

"Well, you can't send him that!" my mother says when she sees it. "What on earth happened to it?"

"I don't know," I say. "I don't know."

It looks so funny that she cannot help from laughing, nor I from crying.

She brings a tape recorder from her apartment and sets it up on my bed. I'm old enough to write letters, as old as twelve perhaps, but I'm supposed to use tapes in lieu of pencil and paper to send messages to my father. She promised him I would. I can push the square red button when I'm ready, she says.

When she grows bored with my unreadiness, she leaves the room. I follow her. I don't want to be left alone with the heavy black box studded with silver knobs. Looking at it, I see a black casket with shiny steel hardware, the kind into which a magician locks a girl before he saws her in half.

I cling to my mother's sleeve, making her angry. We try over and over to induce me to say something into the microphone on the end of the black wire. Nothing works. Not threats, not promises.

My mouth, so uncooperative. At swimming school it opens under the surface of the pool and water rushes in, choking me. In front of the tape recorder, it closes on my tongue, refuses to surrender even one word.

Someday a sentence will come to me, a magic sentence that will undo all that is wrong and make everything right. But until that sentence comes, I say nothing.

It begins when I'm twenty. It begins with a visit, and afterward my mother and I disagree over whose idea it was to invite him. My mother says that it was mine. I think it was hers.

It's been ten years since I've seen him, and if my mother is right—if inviting my father to come see us was my idea—it must be that my curiosity over the hidden parent, the other half of me, is great enough to overcome the discouragement of the letters. Perhaps I suspect or hope that passion lies behind such a bluster of ideology. That something must require such a screen; some interesting beast must be contained by this cage within cage of words.

My parents have shared their secret meetings over the years. In distant cities, and despite another wife and other children, they've said they would run away, remarry, try it again, but their plans always fall through. My mother and father were together for no more than two years, married for less than one, divorced before my first birthday. If I suspect that the coming visit is my mother's idea, it's because I don't remember suggesting it myself, and it has been too long since she's seen him—too long since she's taken any solitary, mysterious vacations.

Perhaps what I later conclude is true: she uses his curiosity about me, and mine about him, as the excuse to plan a reunion that will include her. If this is the case, how bitterly she will come to regret the ruse.

The visit is scheduled for spring break of my junior year in college, exactly a week after my twentieth birthday, which falls, as usual, in the middle of exams.

"So," says my boyfriend, bidding me good-bye in the parking lot outside my dorm. "Pretty heavy."

"Do you think?" I ask. I've carefully not considered the prospect of seeing my father for the first time in ten years, for only the third time in my life. As always, my course load was heavy, and the last weeks were lost to late hours in the library.

"Are you kidding?" he says, and I shrug and look away, a gesture, one among my many, of evasion.

This boyfriend is older than I, a graduate student. He's a gentle person, and the quality affords him a unique position in my brief history of boyfriends. His own father died when he was an infant; he has no stepfather. Having missed his lost father for all of his life, he knows what I cannot admit: that some of the longing in my life must be focused on that hole in the family portraits. It cannot all be consecrated to my mother.

The drive home takes seven hours, hours during which I play the same Rolling Stones album over and over, letting the tape deck's auto-reverse mechanism make a continuous loop of sound. The insistent rhythms consume the miles of gray highway and make deep consideration impossible. My thoughts skip and skid and skitter like the discarded cups and candy wrappers on the windy embankments.

My grandmother's bedroom: the two of us sitting together at the foot of my grandparents' big bed. I'm six, maybe seven. She's just taken a bath. She's wearing a slip and is drawing one of her old-fashioned stockings up over her knee and fastening it to her garter. In her sixties, she still has nice legs. Her skin is a warm olive, smooth and lustrous; her kneecaps, as small and inviting as walnuts, make me want to touch them. As she does every day, she is wearing Chanel No. 5 and the string of pearls her father gave her when she was seventeen.

"Tickle my neck," she says, and I run my fingers lightly over the place where her blacked hair is shorn just at the nape.

"Do you know," I say, "I love you more than anyone else in the world. I love you more than Mommy."

My grandmother takes my hand from her neck. "No," she says. "You don't."

I am silent, chastened by her refusal of what I've given her.

"You love your mother best. That's the way it is for every child, and that's the way it is for you, too."

It's a scrupulous rather than truthful statement from my grandmother. She fully intends that I should love her best—she expects to be everyone's first love—but at the time, many of her arguments with my mother have to do with whether one or the other of them is plotting to alienate my affections. As my mother has recently moved out, perhaps inspiring this pragmatic shift of adoration, my grandmother is careful not to say anything seditious that I might repeat.

I watch as she pulls up her other stocking and fastens it. That afternoon, I begin to learn the wisdom of keeping my feelings to myself, a lesson reinforced often during a childhood of female warfare and tricky, shifting alliances, so often that my genius for evasion at last approaches that of my mother. She may sleep with a mask, but by the time I am a teenager I have made one within myself, I have hidden my heart.

Rebuked by my grandmother, sitting in silence beside her, I begin to teach myself to define what I really feel toward my mother—a desperate, fearful anger over her having abandoned me, an anger that has left me stricken with asthma and rashes—as *love.*

And what about my mother, so ready to use the word, to write me a note comprised of nothing but kiss *X*s and the hollow *O*s of her hugs? Her anger with me is wild and uncontrolled, a force that seems to take her by surprise as much as it does me. Once, just before she moves out, I get underfoot while she is dressing for a date. She is late, and I am irksome. Standing with her before her mirror, I reach under her arm for one of her lipsticks, and she turns on me with her hairbrush. Her blows fall all over me. She chases me down the staircase, hitting whatever she can reach—my back, my legs, the top of my head. At the bottom of the stairs, I collapse in tears, at first in shock and fear, but afterward, when my grandmother and grandfather have come running to the sound of my sobs, I cry with the intention of getting my mother in trouble, cry harder and longer, learning the power of vengeance.

Necklaces. Rings. Clothes. Books. A portable stereo and lenses for my camera. The fountain pen he used in college. His grandfather's razor and strop in its original pewter case etched with curlicues. A diamond stud that belonged to someone—I can't remember who.

Some of his gifts I'll give away, and others I'll sell to a pawnbroker, tearing up the claim check as soon as I'm outside the shop's door. The heirlooms I'll return, packed carefully into a box, insured at the post office and mailed without a letter to his address. They belong to his children. Not me, but the children he raised, the daughters who will still be his when we no longer speak.

Christmas presents. Birthday presents. Presents for Easter, for Valentine's Day, for Halloween. All rewrapped in the pretty paper I am careful not to tear, ribbons I untie but do not cut. I retrieve the bright papers and bows from trash cans after the celebrants of whatever occasion it is have gone to bed. Smooth them, replace them around the boxes. I have to preserve them just so, this evidence of my mother's love, or what passes for it, what she calls love. Her gifts are valuable in that they always provide clues as to how I might ingratiate myself. If she gives me a dress in a size six, then I know to alter my size ten self to fit it. I can make myself the creature she imagines she might love, at least while standing in the store where she buys the dress.

It will be years before I can acknowledge that in preserving such evidence I document another, different emotional transaction: not one of love but of rage, my rage over always receiving directives disguised as gifts and my refusal, ultimately, to accept them. Under the Christmas tree I make the appropriate noises of delight, but then later, alone, after the house is dark, I reverse my response, I reject the gifts by wrapping them back up as if I've never opened them.

It's possible to apply this bifurcated vision to other

areas of my life. An uneasy relationship with food is the standard example in cases such as my mother's and mine. At fifteen, when I stop eating, is it because I want to secure her grudging admiration? Do I want to make myself smaller and smaller until I disappear, truly becoming my mother's daughter: the one she doesn't see? Or am I so angry at her endless nagging me about my weight that I decide I'll never again give her the opportunity to say a word to me about my size. *You want thin?* I remember thinking, *I'll give you thin. I'll define thin, not you.* Not the suggested one hundred and twenty pounds, but ninety-five. And not size six, but size two.

If only I understood the triumph of refusing to eat; if only I could recognize my excitement as that of vengeance, of contriving to shut my mother out, the way that she denied me as I stood for hours by the bed where she lay, her eyes closed and hidden under her mask.

Anorexia may begin as an attempt to make myself fit my mother's ideal and then to erase myself, but its deeper, more insidious and lasting seduction is that of exiling her. Anorexia can be satisfied, my mother cannot; so I replace her with this disease, with a system of penances and renunciation that offers its own reward. That makes mothers obsolete.

A pool party at the big house with the courtyard and the red tile roof, the one owned by the architect she's been dating. It's a house with seven bedrooms, six of them unoccupied. We change in the one he calls "the blue room," an icy pale, female space with a vast canopied bed.

Like boxers, my mother and I back into opposing corners of the bedroom. She's always hated to be seen naked. If she can, she changes in the dark. I watch as she pulls her bathing suit up under her dress, wanting her to look at me, my body. I like nothing so much as taking my clothes off; I do now that I'm so thin. Each day, I undress countless times and stand on the scale. In public restrooms, I wait until I am alone so that I can lift my shirt and admire my ribs in the mirror. Seeing myself is enough to make me gasp with pleasure, to make my hands shake with excitement. I am amazed by this body I've made. I don't interpret it as a criticism that no one else admires it, only as evidence that my standards are too rarefied for ordinary human beings to appreciate. Since I have no boyfriend, there's no one to complain that I've left nothing soft for his hands or his eyes to enjoy.

I am my own lover. At night I go to bed naked, and in the dark I touch my body until I know by heart the map of my hunger.

The dizzy rapture of starving. The power of needing nothing. By force of will I make myself the impossible sprite who lives on air, on water, on purity.

It isn't just appetite for food that I deny, it's all appetite, all desire. It's sex. I starve myself to recapture my sexuality from my mother—not just by making my breasts and hips disappear, but by drying up the blood. The one thing she can't stand about my being so thin is that I don't menstruate: I lose my capacity to get pregnant, to be in a danger of the kind that precipitated the abrupt fall from grace she endured.

Because she's angry, too. She can't have missed hearing the message of my childhood and adolescence, as delivered to me by my grandmother: *Don't make the mistakes your mother made.* How she must hate me, with my good grades and smug avoidance of boys. She has to insist that my transgressing and getting caught is at least possible, and when she discovers that I've lost my period she takes me to doctor after doctor, accompanying me into the consulting room and even the examining room. The gynecologist prescribes hormones, the acupuncturist screws needles into my thighs.

Before I go away to college, we return together to the gynecologist's office. She wants me to get a diaphragm, that notoriously unreliable form of birth control. But I can't be fitted for one.

"Not without breaking her hymen," the doctor says after he examines me. "You don't want to do that, do you?"

My mother, standing near the window, hesitates. I sit up on my elbows. "Yes," she says.

He uses a series of graduated green plastic penises. When he withdraws the set of them from under the lid of a stainless steel surgical tray, I can't believe what I see in his hands. Their green is a green that exists nowhere in nature but that colors surgeons' scrubs and emesis basins and other dire instruments I associate with illness and death. One after another he inserts them, starting with the smallest—no bigger than his little finger—until the second to last one comes out smeared with blood. This doctor deflowers me in front of my mother. Is it because he was her obstetrician, the man who delivered me, that he imagines this is somehow all right?

I lie on the table, a paper sheet over my knees, my hands over my eyes.

Highway repairs and a detour make the drive home from college even longer than usual, and I arrive at my mother's barely in time to sit down for dinner, something French and ambitious to which she must have devoted an afternoon of labor. Even so, we leave the television on during the meal, and taste rather than eat what she prepared.

"You get it," my mother says whenever the phone rings. I find this odd—she's usually so secretive about her social life—but when it rings at nine-thirty, I understand. It's him, my father, calling to give us his flight number. His voice, which I have not heard for ten years, surprises me with its high pitch. I'll learn, in time, that it doesn't always sound this way, but rises and falls in concert with his emotions. On this night, however, we speak only as long as it takes to confirm the necessary details.

"I'll be wearing a brown suit," he says.

"Okay," I say.

"See you soon," he says, ordinary words made extraordinary by the fact that I have never heard them from him, a man I would have seen under other circumstances every day for all the years of my life.

"Okay," I say. "Yes." He's due to arrive at two the next afternoon.

Everything is disrupted for this visit. My mother's companion of many years is banished; I'm not sure where he goes. Perhaps to stay with his estranged wife, the one he can't bring himself to divorce. My grandparents, disapproving, will share one dinner with us at my mother's, one tea at their house. The rest of the week's plans do not include them. I am not sure whether to regard this as a slight, a mercy, or merely a pragmatic consideration of what we all think we might be able to handle together.

My mother and I go to our beds, where we spend our separate, sleepless nights. As only a narrow hallway divides our rooms, we can hear each other sigh and shift beneath the blankets. At one point she gets up. I hear her open and close a drawer in her bathroom.

. . .

My bedroom at my mother's is the first she's ever had for me. She furnished it the summer after I graduated from high school, when, as I was moving from my grandparents' house to college, I would no longer need it. It's a modern room, with a futon whose brightly colored bedding strikes a garish note among the other rooms' understated fugues of beige. The comforter bears a floral pattern of restless, itchy pinks that are echoed in the window blinds. Through them the morning sun streaks in and falls in warm patches on the cream carpet, the pink and cream blending together into a color I associate with inflamed eyelids, epic weeping.

On the wall is a print, a watercolor by Jean-Michel Folon, a painting of a single chair that stands on a hill amidst a grove of leafless trees. The chair is as large as the trees and is in metamorphosis; branches and twigs project from its wooden back. Either it is becoming fully a chair, or it is reverting back to tree. I chose this print with my mother, undoubtedly because it expresses my sense of always striving to become what I am not and because the longing I find expressed in the chair—mute, paralyzed—is also so familiar. Still, despite its beauty, I don't enjoy looking at it. The pink glow coming from behind the hill is too faint to suggest hope: there's no way to know if it's sunrise, sunset, or the light of an approaching fire.

The print is reflected twice, in full-length mirrors on closet doors, and the whole room shines with an optimism neither of us has ever felt about the other. Because most of my school holidays are spent with my grandparents, it's a place of brief visits.

We agree that we have to leave for the airport by one o'clock, but I'm dressed to go long before noon. It's not unusual for me to be ready this early. I'm always too early. I arrive at restaurants whole hours before dinner dates and have to walk around neighboring blocks or wait in nearby stores until I'm merely painfully punctual. I'm helpless against it, this response to my mother's chronic lateness, to having always been the last child to be picked up from school, camp, church, birthday parties, dental appointments, dance lessons.

Always in tears, always sure that this time she wouldn't come at all but would leave me forever with the dentist or the Russian ballet mistress who slapped the backs of my knees with her yardstick. Even after my mother moved out, the arrangement between her and my grandmother was that she would provide at least half of whatever transportation I required; and so in hallways and foyers, on dank stone benches or the vinyl-upholstered couches of waiting rooms, I silently rehearsed my grandparents' phone number and their address, to which the police should return me.

My mother's lateness is so extreme it transcends hostile insult. The reason for lost jobs and lost loves, for useless sessions of behavior therapy, it implies she exists in another temporal frame. In being late, if in little else, my mother is so predictable that my grandmother routinely gives her the wrong time for family gatherings, adjusting it as much as two whole hours forward, and still my mother nearly misses them. But I am not as pragmatic as my grandmother; and I never get used to it.

At 12:45 I knock on the bedroom door. She's out of the bath, she's set her hair, but she has not put on her makeup. She's not wearing anything but a bra and a slip. Discarded blouses and skirts and trousers cover every surface of her usually immaculate bedroom.

Shoes tumble from the closet as if arrested in the attempt to escape. I sit in the rocker and watch her. "That looks nice," I encourage with each change of clothes, but she looks in the mirror and tears whatever it is off.

"Please," I say. "It's one." And then, after a few more outfits, "It's one-fifteen."

"You go," she says. "I can't. I'm not ready." She sits on the bed, still undressed. She puts her face in her hands.

"Alone?" I say. "I can't."

"You'll have to. Or you'll be late."

"Just put something on," I beg. "Please. I'll drive, and you can do your makeup in the car."

"No. You go."

At one-thirty I leave, transfixed with dread, whether of the solitary meeting or of being late, I can't say. I speed on the highway, flooded with adrenaline, nervous enough that my back aches, a cold clench.

I park the car and run all the way from the lot and through the terminal to the gate. I arrive breathing hard. A man wearing a tan suit, not a brown one, straightens slowly from the drinking fountain, and turns to look at me. We recognize one another immediately. We've exchanged recent photographs, but it's more than that: we look like each other.

As my father walks toward me, he wipes his wet mouth with the back of his free hand. The other carries a heavy-looking black case—his camera, he explains. "You're late," he says. Even though the plane was delayed, it has been on the ground for some minutes.

"I know," I say. "I'm sorry. The traffic . . ."

I lie to protect my mother, so naked in her bra and curlers. I could give her away, let him know how much this visit means to her, enough to warrant a frenzied morning before the mirror, but I don't. I protect her, as I've learned to do from her own example, from the mask, the secret phone number. I cannot remember a time that I was not aware of my mother's fragility. It's part of what has convinced me of her surpassing worth, the way only the best teacups break easily.

In the terminal, my father leads me out of the flow of passengers and the friends and family who have come to meet them. He finds an empty spot by one of the big plate-glass windows that look out onto the air-fields. "Don't move," he says. "Just let me look at you."

My father looks at me, then, as no one has ever looked at me before. His hot eyes consume me—eyes that I will discover are always just this bloodshot. I almost feel their touch. He takes my hands, one in each of his, and turns them over, stares at my palms. He does not actually kiss them, but his look is one that ravishes.

"Oh!" he says. "Turn around!" I feel his gaze as it moves over my neck, my back, and down to my feet.

"God," he says when I face him again. "Oh God." His eyes, now fixed on mine, are bright with tears. "Your hair," he says. "It's . . . it's longer than I imagined. Than I could have. It was behind your shoulders in the picture you sent."

I nod. I don't speak. His eyes rob me of words, they seem to draw the air from my mouth so that I can barely breathe.

The girl my father sees has blond hair that falls past her waist, past her hips; it falls to the point at which her fingertips would brush her thighs if her arms were not crossed before her chest. I'm no longer very thin—away at school I've learned to eat—but, as if embarrassed to be caught with a body, I hide whatever I can of it.

We walk to the baggage claim in silence and wait where the metal plates of the luggage conveyor slide one under the other as the stream of suitcases turns the corner. My father picks up his bag and we walk, still without talking, out of the terminal.

Once outside, he takes one of my hands in his. I feel his fingers tremble. "Do you mind?" he says. "Could I?" I don't take my hand away.

"It isn't brown," I say of his suit as we get in the car.

"Yes it is," he says.

"Isn't it more of a tan or a khaki?"

"It's brown."

The trip home from the airport is mostly silent. I can't think of anything to say, and I don't dare do what I want, escape into music on the stereo. Turned sideways in his seat, my father watches me, and his look doesn't allow my hand to reach for the knob. As I drive I make mistakes I rarely make. My hands, wet from nerves, slip on the steering wheel. As we cross an intersection, my foot loses the clutch and I stall the car in traffic.

At home, my mother is wearing the clothes she set out the previous night: black trousers and a cream-colored cashmere sweater that sets off her dark shining hair. She's in high spirits, a little too high perhaps—her laughter sounds shrill to me. On her breast is a small gold miraculous medal, rays of light bursting from the Virgin's open palms. My parents embrace quickly, almost shyly. They kiss each other's closed mouths with their lips thrust forward in prissy, monkey-like puckers.

We try hard to make it work, the three of us together. We sit in the living room and drink iced tea. "At last," one of us says, "a family." Calling ourselves this, saying the words—Who says them? My mother? My father? Do I?—it's meant ironically, but the pain the words bring, the admission of failure, is so intense that afterward no one speaks. My mother breaks away and goes into the kitchen. She returns with a platter of cheeses and vegetables and little sandwiches, her comments arranged with as much care as the food.

We all stare at one another, fascinated, years of observation collapsed into minutes. We catalog similarities, differences. Whose am I? From the neck down

I'm a replica of my mother, but my head resembles his. The line of his jaw is echoed in mine, as are his cheekbones, his ears, his brow. And how mysterious it is that my father and I do the same things with our hands as we talk. I've never had the chance to see his gestures and learn to mimic them.

I watch and listen as my parents begin to argue. They can't reconstruct a year, a season, or even a week from the past without disagreeing. Whatever they talk about—their wedding day, my birth—it's as if my mother and father experienced two separate, unconnected realities, a disjuncture that allows no compromise, no middle ground. The picture that I form of their courtship is one that I have to piece together; no matter how hard I try to make things fit, it will always have the look of an incomplete collage—some details too large, others too small, many missing.

My father takes pictures of my mother and me. An accomplished amateur photographer, he owns a number of large-format cameras and develops his work himself in a darkroom he's set up in his parsonage. I watch as he poses and records images of her, and she watches as he poses me. Though no one counts aloud, I sense that he is careful to make an equal number of exposures of both of us, and that we all keep track of this quantifiable measure of his attention. Then, "How about the two of you together?" he asks, and my mother and I sit next to each other on the hearth.

These pictures of my mother and me are the last I have of us together. As it turns out, they are overexposed; my father never makes individual prints of them, so I have only the proof sheets showing the two of us, our heads inclined, our bodies not touching. Behind my mother and me, visible between our shoulders, are tongues of flame from the gas log. In certain of the poses the fire looks as if it comes from our clothes themselves, as if the anguished expression we each wear is not the smile we intended but the first rictus of pain. As if what my father caught with his camera was the moment when suddenly we knew we'd begun to burn.

The three of us spend much of our week together at art museums and botanic gardens and other tourist attractions. We are drawn to these places of silent staring and confused, enervated wandering because they make us seem and feel less like freaks as we stare in speechless shock at one another. Rather than increasing the strain, the time we spend with my grandparents is a relief in that it diffuses and refracts our attention, filling a few hours with polite, careful conversation about politics and gardening and books we've all read.

Each night at my mother's house we stay up as late as we can, trying to drain sensation from every minute. Whatever I do—peel an orange, tie my shoe, pour water from a pitcher into the dry soil of a houseplant—enthralls my father. I get up to brush my teeth, and he follows me into the bathroom. He leans against the doorjamb to watch as I squeeze the paste from the tube. His scrutiny both excites and exhausts me. How can it be that anyone finds me so interesting?

"Is that the brand you always use?" he says. "Crest?"

I nod. My teeth, as we've observed aloud, match his in shape and color.

"Did you ever wear braces?" he asks.

"No," I say. He nods.

I'm as captivated by him. I've never really known who my father was, and revelation is inherently seductive. There is, too, the fascination of our likeness, that we resemble each other in ways that transcend physical similarities.

"You walk like your father," my mother used to say to me when I was younger. "As soon as you stood up and put one foot in front of the other, I could see it."

"What do you mean?" I'd say. "How?"

"I can't explain it," she'd say. And she wouldn't try. What she said was spoken wistfully sometimes, but mostly it wasn't a compliment. So much of what my mother and her mother seem to regard in me as alien—my bookishness, for example, or my killjoy disinterest in fashion and in what they consider the fun of manicures and facials and going out for high tea in a tea shop—has always been blamed on the other, rogue half of my genes. What a surprise to find that this judgment, which previously struck me as facile, turns out to be correct. In my father I meet someone not only familial but familiar: like myself. Now, my stubborn streak, my willful, marching walk, and the way I frown when I'm thinking—all such traits are not evidence of my separateness but of my belonging.

"Pretty is as pretty does." My grandfather has said these words to me all my life, and since I'm always doing something wrong I know just how ugly I must be.

My grandfather was seventy-one when I was born, and he often took care of me when I was a small child. A tall, remarkably vigorous man, he gardened, he swam, he drove me to school and helped me with my homework.

It was my grandfather who taught me how to ride a bicycle, and in his shirt pocket he kept a small pad of paper on which he wrote pretend traffic tickets when I went too fast on the long driveway or ran into one of his flower beds. The penalties he doled out were usually tasks that I had to perform in order to insinuate myself back into his good graces. This game of make-believe crimes and punishments was one of which I never tired.

I was a tomboy; I tagged after my grandfather, underfoot so often that my first nickname was Shadow, as in "Me and My——." He whistled the old music-hall tune whenever he heard me coming. Because his patience was greater than theirs, my mother and grandmother turned me over to him at bedtime, and sometimes he had to sing for hours until I fell asleep.

Our companionship gave both of us great pleasure—"Oh, you keep him young! You keep him young!" his wrinkled friends said, tweaking my ear or cheek—but everything changed abruptly when I went through puberty.

"You're too big for that now," my grandfather would say, and he'd push me out of his lap. When he hugged me, he didn't let our bodies touch, he made sure that my breasts and hips didn't press against him. I suppose the same thing must have happened to my mother when she turned twelve or thirteen, her flesh announcing to him that she had become sexual and therefore untouchable, and that his rejection as she slipped from childhood into womanhood must have wounded her as it did me.

Born in 1890, my mother's father is a true Victorian. He was raised in houses in which even a table's curved leg was draped, and he has remained squeamish about what he would call our animal nature. My grandmother can be derisive about his prudishness, Victorian mores being to her like a language she can speak but mostly chooses not to. She alludes disparagingly to my grandfather's willful innocence, and when he turns the television off because an ad for a feminine-hygiene product has interrupted the news broadcast, she throws her magazine down in disgust. "Good God!" she cries. "Are you going to leave the world still thinking the stork brought you into it!"

Whatever it is about my father that so draws me to him must have to do in part with the very different ways he and my grandfather respond to my femaleness. As a child of five or of ten, happiest at my grandfather's elbow while he grafted a branch onto a fruit tree or nailed perches to a bird feeder, I couldn't keep my father's attention. During his two brief visits, his eyes passed quickly over me on their way to my mother. But now that I am grown up, my fingernails no longer rough and black with earth from the garden, my once-bobbed hair long, and my flat chest filled out, my father's eyes are fixed on me; he tears his gaze away with reluctance. This kind of besotted focus is intoxicating, especially for a girl schooled in self-effacement and taught that virtue believes more in its ugliness than in its beauty.

One afternoon, when we've returned from a gallery, I fall asleep sitting next to my father on the couch. When I wake up, whole hours later, my head is in the crook of his elbow, like a baby's. I startle, arms jerking in alarm. "I'm sorry!" I say. "I was so tired."

"Oh, no!" my father says. "Please don't apologize! I'm not sorry at all." He looks at me with his hungry eyes. "My arm went to sleep," he says. "I had to go to the bathroom, but I didn't dare move. If it was up to me, I would have sat holding you forever, I would never have woken you.

"They didn't let me hold you," he says. "Not at all. I don't remember that they ever let me. They had you on a schedule. It was sacrosanct, it was absolute. They tolerated no exceptions. They fed you, they changed you, they put you down. If you cried, no one was allowed to pick you up."

By *they* he means the baby nurse, my mother and grandmother. "They didn't even let me say good-bye," he says. He puts his hand under my chin and turns my face toward his.

My mother is watching him. At one point she opens her mouth as if to say something, but then closes it. As my father talks, tears seep into the crow's feet at the corners of his eyes. They don't fall so much as spread into a glittering web over his face, following the fine lines made by the sun, by laughter, by sorrow. I've never seen a man cry before.

My father's eyes: what is it about them? Their color is utterly familiar—the same as mine, the same as my mother's—but they burn like no other eyes I've ever seen before or since. Burn like a prophet's, a madman's, a lover's. Always shining, always bloodshot, always turned on me with absolute attention. Intelligent eyes, enraptured eyes, luminous, stricken, brilliant, spellbound, spellbinding eyes.

I don't know it yet, not consciously, but I feel it: my father, holding himself so still and staring at me, has somehow begun to *see* me into being. His look gives me to myself, his gaze reflects the life my mother's willfully shut eyes denied. Looking at him looking at me, I cannot help but fall painfully, precipitously in love. And my loving him is inseparable from a piercing sense of loss. Whenever I am alone—in my bedroom, the bathroom—I find myself crying, sometimes even sinking to my knees. How am I to endure this new despair? How can it be that I am twenty years old, that I've had to grow up without a father, only to meet him now when it's too late, when childhood is over, lost?

On the last night my father spends with us, I wake after only two hours of sleep. I sit up in bed and find my wristwatch on the nightstand. It's ten minutes before three. My throat is sore as if I'm catching a cold, and I go downstairs for a glass of orange juice. I move quietly so as not to disturb my father sleeping in the den. The thick carpet on the stair treads absorbs my footfalls. As I pass the den's open door, I see that the convertible sofa is empty, my father is not on it. I turn on the lights in the living room just to make sure he's not sleeping on that couch, but already I know where he is: in my mother's bed.

I sit on the carpeted stairs to consider this, their cheating on his current wife and my mother's banished, trusting partner. Do my parents perhaps consider their bond so primary that it is absolute, ungovernable by the dictates that guide more pedestrian relationships? Maybe they believe that they are being faithful only when they're sleeping together, and that other loves are the betrayal. Alone, outside my mother's closed bedroom door, I feel jealous. And, like all children, I discover that I'm squeamish at the thought of my mother and father having intercourse. I'm both fascinated and repelled.

When I turn on the light in the kitchen, I find a cockroach on the counter; rather than kill it, I gingerly and at arm's length place a water glass upside down over the insect—leaving the problem for my mother to resolve in the morning. I dislike insects, and cockroaches in particular have always frightened me.

As I drink the juice, I see the roach circle inside the glass, rising occasionally on its hind legs to touch the clear, smooth, obstructing surface with its forefeet and sensitive antennae. I watch how it must relentlessly search for the seam, the tiny ridge or rill in the glass that might offer some hope of climbing, penetrating, escaping. But there is nothing about the glass that it understands.

The next day, while my mother is taking a shower, my father talks about what happened the previous night. “I heard you,” he says. “I heard you go downstairs.” He leans forward over the breakfast table. “I did it because I had to,” he says. “She asked me.” I say nothing, but we both know that I know what he’s talking about.

He describes their making love not as sacred, the way I’ve imagined it, but as an act of charitable reassurance. He answers a question I never voice. “I didn’t do it because I wanted to,” he says. Humiliated on behalf of my mother, and shocked that he would betray her this way, I look not at him but at my plate.

When it’s time to take my father to the airport, again my mother says she cannot go. She has a headache.

She is flattened by discouragement. This visit, like all his others, has convinced her that she's wasted years on the wrong men, the wrong life. "You drive him," she says. "He seems more interested in your company than in mine, anyway."

As during our previous conversation about getting to the airport on time, I'm sitting in the rocking chair in her bedroom and she is on her bed, her face in her hands. Looking at her, I can't think of any words that might reach across the divide between us. "All right," I say at last, and I kiss her cheek under her closed eyes. "I'll go. You stay."

When I tell my father she's not coming, he smiles. "Oh good," he says. "I'm glad to have you to myself for a little while." He picks up his bags.

"Maybe you should go up and say good-bye," I say, surprised by his callousness, the way he doesn't seem to consider her feelings when she is slain by as little as a glance from him.

In the terminal, he puts down the camera case to embrace me with both arms. "I love you," he says. "God, I love you. I lost you, but now I have you back, and I'll never let you go again." He says the words and he holds me tightly, so tightly. How solid he is, how real. Father. My father. The word made flesh.

"You don't know how I suffered when they sent me away," he says. "You can't imagine the pain of losing you."

He takes my face in his hands and kisses my forehead, my eyes. "How can a daughter of mine be this beautiful?" he murmurs. "When I look at you, I wonder if I, too, must not be handsome."

My father knows he is a good-looking man. He's overweight, and I have to stretch to get my arms around him, but his features—a strong jaw, high cheekbones, and long nose—are good enough to excuse the excess. I smile, but I don't return to him the compliment I suspect he's trying to prompt.

We look at each other. We search each other's faces. "What happens now?" I say, and we make promises that we'll be together again soon.

"In the summer, maybe," I say.

"No," he says. "Sooner. Sooner."

With his hand under my chin, my father draws my face toward his own. He touches his lips to mine. I stiffen.

I've seen it before: fathers kissing their daughters on

the mouth. A friend of mine's father has kissed her this way for years, and I've watched them, unable to look away, disquieted by what I see. In my family, lip-to-lip kisses between parent and child are considered as vulgar as spitting in public or not washing your hands after using the toilet, all of which failures my grandmother would judge as evidence of poor upbringing. She might excuse such kisses from a person raised in an exotic, backward culture, but never from a decent American.

A voice over the public-address system announces the final boarding call for my father's flight. As I pull away, feeling the resistance of his hand behind my head, how tightly he holds me to him, the kiss changes. It is no longer a chaste, closed-lipped kiss.

My father pushes his tongue deep into my mouth: wet, insistent, exploring, then withdrawn. He picks up his camera case, and, smiling brightly, he joins the end of the line of passengers disappearing into the airplane.

How long do I stand there, my hand to my mouth, people washing around me? The plane has taxied away from the gate before I move. Through the terminal's thick wall of glass, I watch it take off, the thrust that lifts its heavy, shining belly into the clouds.

I am frightened by the kiss. I know it is wrong, and its wrongness is what lets me know, too, that it is a secret.

In years to come, I'll think of the kiss as a kind of transforming sting, like that of a scorpion: a narcotic that spreads from my mouth to my brain. The kiss is the point at which I begin, slowly, inexorably, to fall asleep, to surrender volition, to become paralyzed. It's the drug my father administers in order that he might consume me. That I might desire to be consumed.

The route I take from my mother's home back to school is devoid of visual distractions, a straight path cut through flat, dry country. The highway is so old that the asphalt has faded to a pale gray, its cracks painted over with black lines of tar. It's a road that lacks a vanishing point—even when it isn't hot, a mirage of water glimmers at its end.

The Rolling Stones album still plays in the tape deck, over and over and just as loudly as during the previous drive. But everything is different now, and the difference is the kiss. My thoughts return to it obsessively but never adhere.

One kiss. An instant, seemingly discrete and isolated in time, yet paradoxically so, for the kiss has grown. It is like a vast, glittering wall between me and everything else, a surface offering no purchase, nor any sign by which to understand it. I can see past and through it to the life I used to have, but, mysteriously, the kiss separates me from that life.

I can't dismiss the vision of the cockroach I trapped under the water glass, how it circled slowly at first and then faster, faster.

Back at school, there is a specific hour during which I and students whose last names begin with the same letter as mine are supposed to register for classes, and I miss it. There is a makeup registration and then a late registration that carries a penalty fee, and I miss both of those as well.

The three young women with whom I live rush in and out and around me, signing up for classes, buying books, reuniting with friends, retrieving the previous quarter's grades, blue books, term papers.

I sit in a green vinyl-upholstered chair in our communal living area, and do none of what I, as a student, am supposed to do. "What's with you?" my roommates say. "Is anything wrong?" I may have acted in peculiar ways before—I'm sure I have—but I've never just sat. My screwups, historically, have been of an energetic variety.

"I'm fine," I assure them. "Everything's okay."

Eventually they stop asking questions, and the green chair with its back to the wall is where I spend the better part of two weeks, days and nights as well, sleeping upright, my arms encircling my knees. During the day, I keep a novel open in my lap, and if someone passes through the living room—they tend not to settle there now that I've claimed it for my unnamed, inert vigil—I pretend, sometimes, to be reading.

Once late registration is a week behind me, I receive a letter from the office of academic probation. It asks that I make an appointment to discuss my status.

"What's going on?" my boyfriend asks repeatedly, more vocal than my roommates in his concern. "What happened during the break?"

I recount the surface of the visit. I reconstruct it up until the kiss. I say how bereft I feel at having lost what cannot be recovered: twenty years with a father whom I now find I love and who seems to return that love.

My boyfriend's own lost father makes him a sympathetic listener; he seems not just to understand but to share my anguish, and this encourages me to tell him what I haven't told anyone else. "Something weird happened at the airport," I say. We're in his car, parked in the driveway of the little house he rents off campus. "At least I think it was weird. Maybe it wasn't," I finish hopefully.

"What?" he asks.

"Well, my father was saying good-bye. We were saying good-bye in the airport. And he . . . Well, when he kissed me he sort of put his tongue in my mouth. Do you think that's weird?"

"Are you fucking kidding!" my boyfriend yells at me. "I can't believe that! Yes, it's weird! Of course it's weird! It's wrong! Did you tell your mother?"

I shake my head no. I cover my face with my hands.

My boyfriend's outrage forces me farther into secrecy. I realize that what I felt in the car while driving back to school, that the kiss has separated me from everything else, is true. It's not a conceit or an overly dramatic interpretation. As for my mother, she is the last person I would tell about the kiss; she's the one most likely to respond hysterically, even violently. She would prevent me from ever seeing my father again. And I can't not see him again. From the time he left me, my first thought, the one that pushes aside my fears about the kiss, has been *When.*

When will I see him again? When will we be together? He calls each day—the phone's ring summoning me from the green chair even if registration and classes and friends cannot—and we ask each other the same question over and over: *When?*

I take my hands from my face. "I made a mistake," I tell my boyfriend. "I exaggerated. I described it wrong. It wasn't exactly like that. He may have done it by accident." Bit by bit, layer by temporizing layer, I work to obliterate the truth.

My boyfriend, threatened himself by what I revealed, colludes with me in this process. Together we forget what I've said, even as privately I forget what my father did. It is as simple as only denial can be.

Don't think about it, I tell myself, and I don't, but it seems to require an enormous effort of will.

Everything takes more energy than I have. I realize I'm in a kind of shock; a cold, sinking torpor gives it away—a sensation I recognize from a few years before, when I was hit by a car while riding my bike. The position of my body in the green chair, knees drawn protectively up to my chest; the way I can only answer people's questions internally, my voice won't speak the words I hear in my head: these symptoms are the same as when I was lying in the street, unable to talk to the paramedic. But now I retreat from the cause of my shock; I ascribe it to the discovery of my father and its implicit loss, to the grief over all the years we missed, to the unbearable injustice of getting him back when it's too late, I'm all grown-up. I don't let myself wonder if any of what I feel is in response to his kiss. Curled in the green vinyl chair for those two weeks, hugging an old blue afghan, I become one of the people to whom I wouldn't mention such a thing as my father sticking his tongue in my mouth.

• • •

There is an option offered by the university to students who suddenly find they can't be students. It's called "stopping out," to distinguish it from "dropping out." As long as I register again for classes before a full academic year has passed, I can rematriculate without having to reapply to the university.

"Why do you want to do this?" the counselor in the office of academic probation asks. The last time we talked was when my grades were lost through a computer error at the end of the first quarter of my freshman year. As an incoming student, I didn't realize that I hadn't received a pink grade slip in the mail—I never missed what I didn't know I was supposed to get—and I was shocked when my case was described as one of "particular concern" since I hadn't failed just one or two courses but rather had earned *no* units whatsoever during my first quarter. High school valedictorian, child who routinely threw up from nerves before Latin exams, ambitious student who within a week of arriving at college had petitioned the dean to allow me to take an unusually high course load, I spent an hour sobbing in this same counselor's office before the computer glitch was caught and my professors contacted for my grades.

"I'm just having some family problems," I say to him now. "I need a little time to think." My tears, reminding him perhaps of those that proved so hard to stanch before, stop the interview.

"Yes, yes. Of course," he says briskly. "I'll just get the forms."

The university returns my tuition fees and those for room and board, minus a prorated amount representing the two weeks I've wasted. No longer enrolled, I cannot remain in student housing, and so, despite my near paralysis, I have to move out.

I use the refunded money to rent an apartment, a basement room with squat windows forced up to the low ceiling and plumbing tangled like entrails overhead. The pipes sweat and seep, filling the dark space with a uterine warmth. The basement, a labyrinth of dank, linoleum-floored units, is part of an old estate now engulfed by the campus. It borders the student commons, where the bookstore and bank and post office are located, and outside my windows busy feet walk or run by.

The sky is invisible from my room. I can't see past the trees in the rear courtyard. This is the spring that bagworms infest the oaks on campus; and the moths' eggs fill silvery webbed pouches that hang from the branches outside my windows. Stray strands of silk twist in the breeze. I watch them, sitting on the end of my bed.

My father continues to telephone me every day. He calls from his office, waiting until the rest of the church's staff has gone home. We talk for hours every night: a courtship encouraged by the paradoxical intimacy of long-distance calls, the telephone's invitation to say anything, to be more forthcoming, passionate, reckless in ways we might not be if we were meeting face-to-face. Our words about love are, like most people's, unoriginal, unmemorable; but my father and I have a subject more consuming than love: *Her.* Love's object. My mother. His wife.

We're locked in the kind of sympathy for each other that only two people spurned by the same woman could feel. Through her, in thrall to her, spiting her—the person neither of us could ever know or possess—we hold on to each other. She is more compelling than we are, because she always eludes. She is mysterious, whereas we are only too eager to bare ourselves.

With words, my father and I lay open the organs of love. We see from where our blood flows, how fast and how thick, how red. It fascinates us, our capacity for pain. For we are in love with that, too: our suffering, the anguish of the unrequited. Or if we don't love suffering, we don't know who or what we are apart from it. For half of his life and all of mine, we have defined ourselves as those who love *her,* the one who won't love us back.

My father vilifies my mother and her parents. I defend them, but they have hurt me, too. It's a relief to hear someone say that my young, beautiful mother, whom all my friends jealously admire, is a narcissist; that she's selfish and cruel as only the weak can be—because cruelty is all she has to keep herself safe.

My father identifies the dire triangle that my grandmother, my mother, and I form. He says that I protect my mother against her mother; that she passively protects me by offering one generation's distance; and that my grandmother manipulates the two of us, playing one daughter's insecurities off against the other's. He disarms me by naming this triangle even as he steps in to break it by forming a new one: my mother, my father, and me. My father takes the place of my grandmother: one despot steps in for another.

Astonished by his honesty, his perceptivity, I somehow miss what I don't want to see—that my father himself is selfish, a narcissist, dangerous.

While he talks, he sits in his unlit office, feet propped on the desk—he describes the scene for me. I lie curled on my bed, the lights out in my room. In those long hours of dark conversation, we fill in twenty years of history, we interrupt ourselves and each other to say over and over how unbearable is our separation. We say we are both bewildered and even frightened by the force of our feelings—yet how can we stand to remain apart as we have been for so long?

His voice fills the darkness. Nothing like this has ever happened to him before, my father says. His church, his wife, his other children: he tells me he doesn't pay any more attention to them than I do to the rest of my life. He is pushing them away even as I withdraw from my family, my friends, my boyfriend; breaking dates, not answering the phone or knocks at my door. He understands why I've stopped out of school. He even applauds it. His only worry is that it will set my grandparents against him, against us; that they will prevent our becoming a part of each other's lives.

"But we'll face that," he says. "Everyone will have to understand that for now I am your school. I am what you have to learn."

I'm excited by my father's desire to tell me everything about himself. How could I be otherwise, child as I am of a father who vanished and a mother so cool and withholding that she left me no means of contacting her when she moved out?

"I have to see you again," he says each night on the phone. "I have to figure out a way to see you again soon. I can't wait much longer."

Then, one night, he calls to say he has a plane ticket. His church will sponsor a trip to the university, where he'll meet with a professor of religion. The money comes out of a fund for the pastor's continuing education. He'll be with me in two weeks.

Before my father arrives, I go home to explain why I've stopped out of school. My grandparents make the connection: as soon as my father reappears, I begin to mismanage my life.

"Drop out!" they protest. "How can you! Why?"

"Stop out, not drop out," I correct, but this distinction is lost on them.

Do my grandparents disapprove of my father's returning for another visit because they suspect that he might be angry enough to be vengeful? Are they frightened that he's coming back because he is at last strong enough to settle the score? To reclaim or destroy all that was his?

"You don't even know him!" my grandmother cries, livid when I tell her that I want to see him again. "He's never even been a father to you!" she says.

"But that's exactly why seeing him has been such a shock. It's why I need to see him again. Why I need to take a break. I need to know who he is."

I cannot answer my grandmother's questions about so sudden an attachment, my willingness to love a person I don't even know. It's a question I can't answer for myself.

"I swear I'll go back in September," I say, and I assure her that having entered college with advanced placement credits and having taken the maximum course load every quarter, I'll still be able to graduate with my class. "Have I ever broken a promise before?" I ask.

My grandfather shakes his head with the same disgust he reserves for my mother's financial mismanagements. He looks at the paper on which I've calculated my credits the way he regards one of her worthless IOUs. "Well," he says, "you've already done it, haven't you? It's not as if you're asking for my opinion, much less my permission."

"I'm sorry," I say to him. "I'm very sorry. I will go back. I promise."

Lips pursed in disapproval, he nods, says nothing. The distance that has long separated his body from mine grows wider.

"Why won't you throw that awful thing out?" my mother says of my favorite black sweater, its embroidery unraveling and dropping jet beads on her kitchen counter. We talk together as we make tea on her stove, and she nods when I tell her that I love my father with a sudden and irresistible force. Depressed in the wake of his visit, she's actually more understanding than my grandparents of my desire to see him again; she is for now, at least.

"Yes! Yes!" she says, when I tell her that he's returning, and we agree that the visit will, once again, include her, that my father and I will drive from school to her house.

My mother looks at me. “Your father is the only man I’ve ever really cared about,” she says. I’ve heard this before, of course, but the confession that follows is new.

“You know, I’ve never really enjoyed being with any other man,” my mother says. “In bed, I mean.” She puts her hand on my arm; she grasps it so that I can feel the separate pressure of each finger. “Having sex is what I mean,” she says, and then she removes her hand, she crosses her arms.

I say nothing. Embarrassed, I look away.

Standing so close that I can feel the heat of her body, can feel her breath as it moves over the fine hairs on my upper arm, I don’t yet know what my mother’s revelation means to me. I feel a tiny cold thrill that I ascribe to the surprise of her willingly telling me something so personal.

Why are you telling me this, I think, marveling silently. *Why?*

Innocent of how I, and my father, will come to use it.

In preparation for my father's visit, I tidy my basement apartment, I borrow an old sleeping bag from a friend. If I worry that he'll dislike the place where I live, so different from my mother's cool and elegant home, I need not. When he gets there, he never sees it. He sees nothing but me.

"Mine," he says, holding me with hands that are hot and shaking. "You belong to me."

He cannot keep from touching me, looking at me, reaching for my hand, my sleeve, my hair. In restaurants, his food grows cold as he stares across the table, his hand holding tight to mine. Tears gather behind the lenses of his glasses and fall silently down his cheeks. They convince me that what I want to believe is true: his love is genuine.

At night I give him my bed. I take the sleeping bag unrolled on the floor beside it.

"That can't be comfortable," he says, but he does not offer to trade places.

"Come here," he says, patting the blanket. "There's room for us both." Remembering the kiss, I hesitate. I'm not ready to have to forget something else.

Is it because he senses I'm troubled by what happened that he's never mentioned our parting in the airport? I think of the kiss not as *what he did* but as *what happened.* I've separated him from the act; I've made the adjustment of regarding the kiss as I would a more helpless physical transport, a seizure, perhaps, or a spasm of coughing. If the kiss was an accident, outside of human control, then it doesn't pollute the love he has for me. It doesn't demand that I turn away from what I want.

Still, I worry. I think about the kiss all the time, but each time I consider asking my father about it, I find I can't open my mouth. It's not just that I'm afraid he might tell me what I don't want to hear, but that I'm so thoroughly under the spell of my own denial I sometimes wonder if anything happened at all. I ask myself if I haven't perhaps made the whole thing up, an overwrought fantasy inspired by wanting too much to be admired and loved.

"Come here," he says again.

I stay where I am, on the floor at his feet, zipped into the bag, caught between fear and longing.

"Please," he says. "I just want to hold you. Don't you want me to? Think of how many years of each other's company we've missed. I don't want to miss any more, do you?"

I want to be held too much to stay away. But, once next to him, I fall asleep before his arms are around me. I sleep above the covers and in the sleeping bag, and in the morning, I rise and bathe before he's awake.

My father began to take photographs, he tells me, to compensate for what he describes as his lack of imagination. He always travels with a camera because without its help he can't visually recall where he's been. He says he can't picture things in his head, that he thinks only in words, a text unrelieved by any sensual memory. Trying to understand what he means, I remember looking something up in the *Encyclopedia Britannica* and noticing how claustrophobic its dry pages were, many crammed only with black letters, no images, the narrowness of the margins discouraging a reader's drifting off into mental pictures. Can it be true that this is what it's like inside my father's head? An endless march of articulation? Not a face or a flower or a room he once slept in, not the smell of sweat or of rain, not the taste of an orange, of wine, of blood—only words and more words?

Between the university and my mother's house are countless scenic stops: lookout points, chasms, rock formations, gulches carved by rivers, gnarled, ancient roots holding tight to big rocks, cliffs above distant roiling water. We take our time as we explore each one, setting a pattern we'll follow for the next few years: my father and I by the side of a road, looking, ostensibly, at some sight worth the drive, but in truth wholly absorbed with each other.

"Sit here," he says, posing me on a rock.

"Do you want me to smile?" I ask.

He looks up from the camera in his hands. "I just want you to be yourself," he says.

I say nothing, and he reaches forward, touches my cheek. "Do you know who you are?" he asks. "How can you, when you're only twenty?"

He stands back and puts the camera before his eyes. "I'll have to show you who you are," he says. "I'll have to do it with this." The shutter clicks, and clicks.

My father takes hundreds of photographs of me. He has to have them, he says, because when I am not before his eyes, it's as if I don't exist. He can't summon my face.

From a mother who won't see me to a father who tells me I am there only when he does see me: perhaps, unconsciously, I consider this an existential promotion. I must, for already I feel that my life depends on my father's seeing me.

I was eleven years old when my grandmother's Persian cat had a litter of kittens. There were five of them, all female, white, perfect. She promised one of them to me, whichever one I wanted. "But don't touch them," she said. "Wait until they're older. Until their eyes open."

Each day I knelt beside the box where they lay with their mother. I picked them up one at a time, cupped each body like milk in my hands and held it so close that I smelled its sweet breath, felt its heart beating under my lips. Eyes sealed, its head bobbed in confusion, bumped my cheek, my chin.

It was one day after school that I did it. I didn't know why, I knew only that I couldn't stop myself. I couldn't bear to see their always sleeping faces, their tiny eyes that never woke to me. For a week, longer, I'd held their beating, blind life in my hands, and I'd felt my heart squeezed in my chest. I'd felt as if I were dying.

I laid one in my lap and, with one thumb on the upper lid, the other on the lower, I carefully pulled its eyes open, separating one delicate membrane of flesh from the other. My heart was pounding and I was sweating with fear, but I accomplished the violation gently. The kitten made no sound, it did not struggle. What I did hadn't seemed to cause it any pain.

I held it up to see its eyes—bleary, watering, already closing against the light. Its head moved in the same blind bobbing circles as before.

Having failed once, I didn't spare the remaining four kittens, I couldn't stop myself from continuing. I finished the job weeping, and the fur around all of the kittens' eyes was wet as well. They looked as exhausted and grief-stricken as I felt, and they curled into their mother's warm belly and went to sleep.

Within a day their eyes were swollen shut, tightly resealed under lids that showed red beneath the fine white fur. I picked one up and tried to brush away the yellow crust that had formed in the corner of one of its eyes. A worm of pus shot out, and, shocked, I dropped the kitten.

I knew this was the worst thing I had ever done, too awful to confess, and when I told my grandmother that I thought something was wrong with the kittens' eyes, I didn't tell her what, only that they looked funny to me. My voice shook as I talked to her.

"What's wrong with you?" she said.

"Nothing," I said. "My throat is sore," I lied.

The veterinarian kept the cat and the kittens for a week. When they returned, their eyes were open and clean, a pale icy blue: disdainful, disinterested. I pulled a string on the floor and they followed it.

"But I thought you wanted one," my grandmother said when they were older, when she was selling them.

"I don't," I told her.

"Why not?"

"I just don't, that's all. I changed my mind."

On our way to my mother's, the backseat of the car filled with camera equipment, my father and I have our first fight, one that begins, like most lover's quarrels, with a misunderstanding as absurd as it is revealing. On a street corner outside a little bistro where we ate dinner, we argue about the price of shampoo. He insists that at some point during his previous visit, I spent thirty dollars on a bottle of shampoo.

"I never!" I say. "Are you kidding! Thirty dollars?"

"I watched you."

"It must have been three dollars. When was it? Where?"

"I saw you hand the cashier the money."

"Look," I say, feeling the shift in the conversation: it's gone from trivial to deadly serious. "In my entire life I have never spent more than four dollars on shampoo, and that was a very big bottle."

"But you did," he says, his face red. "I saw you."

"Come on. Not even my mother would spend that much on shampoo. I don't even think it's possible."

We pursue the topic, ridiculous, essential, until we are too exhausted to continue. Nothing I say will convince him of the truth. But, at twenty, I am still in the throes of rebelling against my mother's extravagance. I wear thrift-store sweaters, army surplus trousers, and when I buy shampoo, I ostentatiously spend a dollar fifty-nine on a tube of Prell in response to my mother's ten-dollar vials of Klorane, her five-dollar, half-ounce applications of rare, cuticle-smoothing emollients. Twenty years past his humiliation by my family, years spent in feverish accomplishment—two master's degrees and one doctorate from top universities, followed by a notably quick ascension through the ranks of his church—my father is still stinging. To me he ascribes my mother's waste of money, and for it he punishes me. And when I at last give in, it isn't only because our argument is pointless and unresolvable.

"Okay," I say. "Okay, you're right," deciding that in this small way I can atone for his being shamed by the people who raised me. After all, I know how foolish, how frail and mistaken my mother and grandmother can make a person feel.

My father tells me that his ordination was postponed by mandatory psychoanalysis, and I am not as interested in this confession as I should be. I want my father to be perfect. The details he offers are scant. In one of the small towns where he served as a traveling pastor—in the days he described to me when I was ten and chose a barn to paint for him—he put his fist through a church wall.

Damned by his gifts as much as by his misfortunes, my father's intelligence is itself an enemy. The mind that fascinates me with its nimbleness, its elastic capacity, could outwit most psychiatrists. It can't have taken him long to perceive which behaviors and opinions were appropriate to a minister and which ones he had better keep to himself. If therapy was useful to him, it was that in its context he learned how to create a desirable profile for a pastor, even if, as he says to me, he has "unresolved problems with the church."

In spite of those conflicts, my father needed badly enough to succeed on the world's terms—to prove my grandparents wrong in their harsh dismissal of him—that by force of will he accomplished all he did with his rage intact, his hurt as sharp as mine, and directed against the same person as mine.

The greatest blindness we share, my father and I, is that neither of us knows how angry we are. It's perhaps because I cannot admit my fury that I don't see what he hides from himself. And he, long practiced in self-deception, doesn't see my anger either.

Whatever passions we feel, we call love.

We're late arriving at my mother's, where we discover that the hard-won, precarious balance of our threesome, our "little family," has been undone.

My father no longer makes the gesture of taking one photograph of my mother for every one of me; and not only his camera has shifted its focus. In my mother's home, both of us her guests, my father and I forsake her, our former object of devotion, for each other. All that the three of us did together in relative comfort on the previous visit—trips to galleries to look at art, trips to gardens to look at plants, to restaurants to look at each other—has become awkward, and quite literally so. We bump into one another; we step on each other's feet; we knock over flowerpots.

My father is an unsettling presence in my mother's living room, where objects are carefully chosen and placed, surfaces immaculate, where the protocol is that emotions remain veiled, postures chaste. Even when he is silent, his features composed, my father's heavy white flesh conveys a voluptuous sorrow in the gravity it demands. It's as if his weight were more a psychic than a physical burden. His arms are fat like a boy's, and his corpulence makes him not sexless but androgynous, adding female to the male. His limbs are large and strong but their muscles are cloaked with fat, their strength hidden by it. And while he isn't grossly overweight—in suits he appears big rather than obese—beneath the thin fabric of his shirt a heavy man's breasts are disconcertingly visible. His large hands are beautiful the way men's rarely are, each finger straight, strong, manicured; and his fleshy feet are pampered as well, the gracefully formed toenails smoothly filed. We joke about how much prettier are his feet than mine or my mother's.

For women like my mother and myself, careful listeners to society's normative messages of beauty and gender, a body such as my father's and his utter lack of self-consciousness over it are as subversive and disquieting as is his readiness to weep. Everything about my father bespeaks appetites satisfied, hurts soothed. In contrast to my own flesh, always silenced, its hunger and pain ignored, his—so white, so indolent—both fascinates and repels me. I find my eyes return again and again to the dark points of his nipples. How different they are from the shriveled coins of college boys', their hard chests, lean bellies.

At meals, when my father bites into buttered bread or a banana or even something as yielding as yogurt, I can hear his teeth come together. They meet with a little snap, and I shudder at this noise that betrays the force of his hunger, and that reminds me of my own. Of a lifetime of hidden, thwarted desire.

This time, when I return to my mother's house after taking him to the airport—no kiss, instead a feverish, disheveled embrace—she is pacing around the white couch in her living room.

"There's something wrong with all of this," she says. "I feel it."

I sit down on the couch, exhausted, tear-stained. "Wrong with what?" I say, betraying my impatience, my unwillingness to be forced to defend myself, or him.

"You know," she says, "he isn't normal. Your father is not a normal person."

"He isn't?" I say. "What do you mean?"

I don't want to have this conversation. I don't want

to have conversations with anyone but my father, and my mother is angry, I can tell. She has that stiff prowl, all of her held in tight control except for her dark, darting eyes.

"Anyway," I say, "who *is* normal?" It's a retort that, much later, my father will throw at me.

"I don't know. I'm just uneasy about this. You're . . . you're fixated on each other. I mean, I understand it in you—you've never had a father. Anyone would expect you to be mesmerized. But him—" My mother stops and turns.

"You know," she says, pointing, "this isn't about *you.* It's about *me.*"

By "it"—and I know this right away, there's nothing more clear than this usually vague little word—she means the love my father professes, the trembling hands and hot eyes. All of what she has noticed and is frightened by. So inappropriate, so immoderate.

So abnormal to love me so completely: that's what I hear her say. What I hear is that not only does my mother not love or admire me, but she will find a way to reinterpret my father's love, to make it all her own.

She folds her arms and looks at me. I look away. I

won't let her see with what deft strokes she can cut the very ground from beneath my feet.

By claiming all of my father's devotion, she pushes me toward him. Because, if she won't love me, then the only way not to fall into the abyss of the unloved is by clinging to him.

"Don't you see?" she insists. "Can't you see that I'm right?"

I don't answer. No, I don't see. I won't.

Years after my mother's death, I'll know that she was right. I'll read letters my father sent to her when she was eighteen, nineteen, twenty: seventy-six of them stored in a Charles Jourdan shoe box, the last of which is dated October 22, 1970, and invokes the word *love* in all but one sentence.

I'll read the letters through and then read them again. Like all children, I'll be compelled forever by my parents' courtship. But what will fascinate me about the letters my father sent my mother will not be any quaint "otherness," not their belonging to a time different from my own, but their absolute familiarity. I'll have read letters just like them: letters addressed to me. The ones written to me are written in the same language, the language of desire, of possession. The ones to me include identical lines from poems and songs.

I'll weep reading the letters my father sent my mother, for all that is in them, all that I so wanted to believe was mine and only mine was, as she said, hers.

In my basement apartment, my life is one of idle enervation. The research projects I outline to my grandparents, the reason for remaining on campus and spending their money on rent, are a sham. My time, empty of activity, is filled by my father. I think of no one else, of nothing else.

It is April. It is May. Days pass unmarked, except in relation to how long it is since last we were together and how long it will be before we're together again. Neither of us is satisfied with anything less than the total possession of the other. My father doesn't care if he has interrupted my education or cut me off from my friends; he delights in any evidence of my enslavement to him. And I never consider his work or his family, the money spent on phone bills and airfares instead of on his children's clothing.

I have embarked on a peculiar passage in my life—a time out of real time, one which will not fit either into the life I lived as a child or the one I create as a woman, but which will carry me, like a road, from one to the other.

"You were named for saints and queens," my mother told me when I was young enough that a halo and a crown seemed interchangeable. We weren't Catholics yet. We were members of the First Church of Christ, Scientist. Above my bed was a plaque bearing these words from its founder, Mary Baker Eddy: "Father-Mother Good, lovingly thee I seek. In the way thou hast, be it slow or fast, up to thee."

The little prayer, which I was taught to recite as I fell asleep, scared me. I didn't want to die fast. As every asthma attack I had seemed capable of killing me, when I wasn't thinking of my mother I thought of death and of God. They made my first trinity: Mother, Death, God.

By the time I was born, all that survived of my grandparents' Jewishness was that our household was pervaded by a sense of *clean* and *unclean, chosen* and *unchosen.* My mother never went to temple, and I think the faith of her forebears must have struck her as dowdy and workaday, lacking the overt glamour of crucifixion. The blood of Judaism was as old and dull as a scab, whereas Christ's flowed brightly each Sunday.

I might have remained immune to the mind-over-matter doctrines of Mrs. Eddy if I had not, when I was six, suffered an accident that occasioned a visit to a Christian Science practitioner, or healer. Since my mother had moved out, my grandfather drove me to school in the morning, a ride that was interrupted dramatically the day the old Lincoln's brakes failed.

Pumping the useless pedal, my grandfather turned off the road to avoid rear-ending the car ahead of us. We went down a short embankment, picked up speed, crossed a ditch, and hit a tree. On impact, the door to the glove compartment popped open; and, not wearing a seat belt, I sailed forward and split my chin on its lock mechanism, cracking my jawbone.

My grandfather was not hurt. He got me out of the wrecked, smoking car and pressed a folded handkerchief to my face. Blood was pouring out of my mouth and chin, and I started to cry, from fear more than pain. I was struggling against this makeshift compress when, by a strange coincidence, my mother, en route to the law office where she worked as a secretary, saw us from the street and pulled over. Her sudden materialization, the way she sprang nimbly out of her blue car, seemed to me angelic, magical, an impression enhanced by the dress she was wearing that morning, one with a tight bodice and a full crimson skirt embroidered all over with music notes. Whenever she wore this dress I was unable to resist touching the fabric of the skirt. I found the notes evocative, mysterious, and if she let me, I traced my finger over the stitched dots as if they represented a different code than that of music's, like Braille or Morse, a message that I might in time decipher.

My mother was unusually patient and gentle as she helped me into her car. We left my grandfather waiting for a tow truck and drove to a nearby medical center, where I was x-rayed and prepared for suturing. I lay under a light so bright it almost forced me to close my eyes, while a blue disposable cloth with a hole cut out for my chin descended over my face like a shroud, blocking my view of my mother. I held her hand tightly, too tightly, perhaps, because after a moment she pried my fingers off and laid my hand on the side of the gurney. She had to make a phone call, she said, she had to explain why she hadn't shown up at work.

I tried to be brave, but when I heard my mother's heels click away I succumbed to animal terror and tried to kick and claw my way after her. All I understood was that she was leaving me again—this time with strangers—and it took both the doctor and his nurse to restrain me. Once they had, I was tranquilized before I was stitched and then finally taken home asleep. Later that afternoon, I woke up screaming in a panic that had been interrupted, not assuaged, by the drug. My mother, soon exhausted by my relentless crying and clinging to her neck, her legs, her fingers—to whatever she would let me hold—took me to a practitioner whose name she picked at random from the listings in the back of *The Christian Science Journal.*

The practitioner was a woman with gray hair and a woolly, nubby sweater that I touched as she prayed over me, my head in her lap and one of her hands on my forehead, the other over my heart. Under those hands, which I remember as cool and calm, even sparing in their movements, I felt my fear drain away. Then the top of my skull seemed to be opened by a sudden, revelatory blow, and a searing light filled me.

Mysteriously, unexpectedly, this stranger ushered me into an experience of something I cannot help but call rapture. I felt myself separated from my flesh, and from all earthly things. I felt myself no more corporeal than the tremble in the air over a fire. I had no words for what happened—I never will have—and in astonishment I stopped crying. My mother sighed in relief; and I learned, at six, a truth dangerous to someone so young and so lovelorn. I saw that transcendence was possible: that spirit could conquer matter, and that therefore I could overcome whatever obstacles prevented my mother's loving me. I could overcome myself.

Every day the sun rises and sinks over the Grand Canyon, each time filling it with shadows the color of blood. On the road we are free, and yet it is a freedom too exhausting to sustain. There's no place to light or to rest, and though for now it goes unrecognized, denied, there will always be the knowledge that what we felt during our first stricken week together is the truth: We lost each other. We lost my childhood and his fatherhood and twenty years of love, and these losses are not recoverable. We are fleeing from this truth, but we can't flee indefinitely.

After months of letters and calls, as many as three of each in a day, all promising devotion, all asking for mine, my father has prepared me for what he requests.

"I'm not sure I want to," I say. "I don't think I can." My teeth chatter in the warm car.

It's dusk when he finally says it. The canyon is dark. The canyon is a river of blood, because when my father says the words I've dreaded—"make love" is the expression he uses—God's heart bursts, it breaks. For me it does.

"I love you," my father says. "I need you."

"I need you, too," I whisper. Please don't make this the price, I beg silently.

"What are you afraid of?" he asks.

I'm afraid that whatever he wants, I will give him. It's only a matter of time. "Going to hell," I say, not really joking.

He laughs to tell me I'm being childish, naive. In his laugh are all his years of studying theology held up against my ignorance of whatever God and His anger might be like.

"There are rules that apply to most people," says my father, "and there are people who are outside of those rules. People who are—"

"How can you know that you—that we—are exceptions?"

"I just do," he says. "You'll have to trust me."

My father and I argue about the nature of love and its expression. These conversations begin like academic papers with suffocating theories, Latin and Greek words from divinity school: *agapē, caritas.* Not *erōs.* But then abruptly they devolve into the personal. How can he help the way he feels for me? It's the way God made him.

"God gave you to me," he says.

When the preacher in my father speaks, I lose what's left of my power to defend myself. The words that might send most people running are the very words to trap me.

God gave you to me. Does my father believe this? He convinces me that he does, that I am his by ordained right, his to do with what he wants. It doesn't occur to me that his invocation of divine will is the tidiest and most unassailable means of exonerating us both. I never question his sanity; although I will come to the point where it is less painful to regard my father as crazy than to conclude that he has been so canny in his judgment of my character and its frailties that he knows exactly what language to use, what noose of words to cast around my neck.

In the years following the car accident, and with increased fervor after the debacle of the French test, I became determined to return to wherever it was I had visited in the practitioner's lap, and I thought this place might be discovered in Sunday school. Around the wood-laminate table I was the only child who had done the previous week's assignment, who had marked my white vinyl-covered Bible with the special blue chalk and read the corresponding snippet from Mary Baker Eddy's *Key to the Scriptures.* The other children lolled and dozed in clip-on neckties and pastel-sashed dresses while I sat up straight. The teacher had barely finished asking a question before my hand, in its white cotton glove buttoned tight at the wrist, shot up. Sometimes I saw the teacher looking at me with what seemed even then like consternation. The lassitude of the other children, their carelessly incorrect answers that proceeded from lips still bearing traces of hastily consumed cold cereal were clearly what she expected. What was disconcerting was my fierce recital of verses, my vigilant posture on the edge of the red plastic kindergarten chair.

The arena of faith was the only one in which I had a chance of securing my mother's attention. Since she was not around during the week to answer to more grubby requirements, and because she was always one who preferred the choice morsel, it was to my mother rather than to my grandparents that the guidance of my soul was entrusted. On Sundays, after church, we went to a nearby patio restaurant, where we sat in curlicued wrought-iron chairs and reviewed my Sunday school lesson while eating club sandwiches held together with toothpicks. The waiters flirted with my mother, and men at neighboring tables smiled in her direction. They looked at her left hand, which had no ring. They seemed to share my longing for my mother—who already embodied for me the beauty of youth, who had the shiny-haired, smooth-cheeked vitality my grandparents did not have, who could do backbends and cartwheels and who owned high-heeled shoes in fifteen colors—who became ever more precious for her elusiveness.

I grew impatient with *Key to the Scriptures,* and in order to reexperience the ecstatic rise that had for an instant made me an attractive child and that came through the experience of pain, I began secretly to practice the mortification of my flesh. At my grandfather's workbench, I turned his vise on my finger joints. When my grandmother brought home ice cream from Baskin-Robbins and discarded the dry ice with which it was packed, I used the salad tongs to retrieve the small smoking slab from the trash can. In the privacy of the upstairs bathroom, I touched my tongue to the dry ice's surface and left a little of its skin there. I looked in the mirror at the blood coming out of my mouth, at the same magic flow that had once summoned my mother from the impossibly wide world of grown-ups and traffic and delivered her to my side. Through those transformations made possible by faith, I would become worthy of her loving me. Either that, or faith would make me feel no more pain from my mother's abandonment than I did from my jaw while lying in the practitioner's lap.

So I looked in the mirror at my tongue, I tasted my blood, and I practiced not hurting.

My mother converted to Catholicism when I was ten, and I followed in her wake, seeking her even as she sought whatever it was she didn't find in Christian Science. In preparation for my first communion, I was catechized by a priest named Father Dove. Despite this felicitous name, Father Dove was not the Holy Spirit incarnate: he chain-smoked, and the face over his white collar had a worldly, sanguinary hue. In a repetition of failures not unlike those of my humiliating French career, I frustrated the priest and angered my mother by consistently answering one question incorrectly. "What is it that becomes the body and blood of Christ?" Father Dove wanted to know.

"Bread and water," I said every time, substituting prisoner's fare for the holy meal of the Eucharist. In the end, since it was the only question among the fifty that I couldn't get right, he passed me.

Nevertheless, "A distressing mistake," he said, looking at me and my mother through the veil of cigarette smoke. "I trust it doesn't mean anything."

For Christmas I received a boxed set of *Lives of the*

Saints. There were two volumes of male saints, which I read once and then left in a drawer, and two of female saints, which I studied and slept with. The books included color plates, illustrations adapted from works of the masters. Blinded Lucy. Maimed Agatha, her breasts on a platter. Beheaded Agnes. Margaret pressed to death under a door piled high with stones. Perpetua and Felicity mauled by wild beasts.

And Dymphna, patroness of those suffering mental illness. Dymphna was the daughter of a widowed Irish king who wanted to marry her. She fled, but he pursued her. She refused him, and he cut off her head.

My father is a brilliantly clear theologian, as only arrogance could make him. His faith is comprised of answers, no uncertainties. Meeting me is what he characterizes as the first crisis of that faith: in me he found a creature more worthy of worship than the Creator. He was frightened when he felt he loved me more than God, but the heresy was resolved when God announced to my father that He was revealing Himself to my father through me.

"God did?" I say. "How do you know?" I cover my

face as I talk, I cannot look at him. His words about God make me dizzy, almost sick. They frighten me more than anything he could say about sex. How can he claim such an ally? How can I defend myself if he does? The god he has must be different and stronger than mine, who died in the canyon.

This time, when we return to our separate homes, I am relieved. The constant calls and tapes and letters assure me that my father is as much mine long distance as he is in person, and without the complications of staving off his physical advances, and denying my own response to them.

Alone in my apartment, I receive no guests, I rarely go out. Having stopped out of school, I've lost contact with my friends: I've withdrawn from them, and they from me. Though my relationship with my father has not been consummated, it is unnatural, and observably so. How pale we are when we're together, and then, in the next instant, how flushed; how our hands shake; how we weep without provocation. Consumed by my father, I hide myself in my underground room. On the few occasions that I see someone approach through my squat windows or hear footfalls in the long corridor outside my door, I don't answer the bell. Instead, I crouch on the floor between my bed and the wall until whoever it is leaves. Sometimes I fall asleep there, my arms around my knees, my body curled tight.

For as long as I know my father, no matter where I live, I will always be in a room like this one—cramped, uncomfortable. No matter what floor it is on, it will be bathed in this dim, drowned light.

My attempts to escape the basement are few and unsuccessful. I spend a token night or two with my boyfriend and return to find my phone already ringing.

"Where were you!" my father demands, nearly hysterical, spluttering in anger.

"I was out," I say.

"With him?"

"Yes. Him."

Our quarrels about the boyfriend are not honest in that what we talk about is whether he is worthy of me, not whether my father is jealous of him. And though I don't reassure my father—I won't give him the satisfaction, nor will I relinquish the facade of independence—my relationship with my boyfriend has not survived my father's sudden entry into my life. In a few months, my boyfriend will move away. We won't break up, exactly. Instead, we'll allow his being hired for a job in a far-off city to redefine us as a long-distance couple, this geographic estrangement a useful way to excuse the alienation we continue to suffer in the long wake of the kiss.

Apart from my boyfriend, my closest female friend is the only person I see; and we don't talk about my father. The changes wrought in me over the past months have been so profound and, perhaps on a level neither of us can acknowledge, so worrisome that we always find some subject other than what is happening to me. I am beginning to learn what it means: *unspeakable.*

And yet, for as long as we live, we express ourselves. With or without words, we speak. There are stories of mad people, of people possessed: on their bodies writing appears to tell of the anguish they hold inside. In an earlier century, a case of shingles might have been cause for exorcism.

The skin on my neck breaks out in blisters, each the size of a match head and clustered in patches of twenty or more that open to form raw sores. Before a week passes, the "lesions," as the doctor calls them, have spread onto my shoulder, my back, my chest, and down my right arm all the way to the tip of my thumb. The infection follows nerve paths that originate from my seventh cervical vertebra, where herpes zoster, the chicken-pox virus, has lain dormant since I contracted it, at age five.

What a memory the body has, events recorded in our bones, our blood, our nerves. It was the summer of my father's first visit, just after he left, that I came down with chicken pox.

"But why would it become active now?" I ask the doctor on my second visit. "Why now, after fifteen years?"

"Stress," he says. "Physical or emotional stress." He raises his eyebrows meaningfully at me. "What's happening in your life?" he asks.

"Oh," I say. "Not much." I tell him that I'm moving out of my apartment, that I'll be traveling during the summer and returning to college in the fall.

"You're underweight," he says. "Are you eating properly, taking your vitamins?"

"Oh, yes," I say.

"What about sleep? Do you sleep well?"

"Yes. Fine."

He frowns. He knows I must be lying. I can't turn my neck. My right arm is so weak I can't use it; and my right hand, the one with which I write and eat—hand of volition, of purpose—can't close around a pencil or a spoon, can't make a fist. The pain of shingles is worse than any other I've experienced, so bad that dressing myself requires an hour, during which I take breaks to cry.

There's no cure for shingles, not in 1981; the drug that suppresses the virus is not yet available. My case will have to run its course. The doctor gives me another cortisone shot for the pain, and prescriptions for topical medications and poultices to help dry up new blisters before they break and become vulnerable to local bacterial infections.

"Maybe you should postpone your trip," my mother says when she sees me, my arm in a sling, a whiplash collar around my neck. My father and I have planned to meet in the city where he was born. I've had the plane tickets for weeks, long before I got ill.

"No," I say. "I want to go." And I do. As frightened as I am to be with my father, I can't not see him. My need for him is inexorable. I can't arrest it any more than I could stop myself from falling if, having stepped from a rooftop into the air, I remembered, too late, the fact of gravity.

On this visit my father has promised to show me the house he lived in as a boy, his missionary grandparents' house with walls three feet thick. We'll eat at the diner where he ordered malts; we'll drive past his old grade school, and we'll walk around the campus of the university he attended after he and my mother were divorced: we'll find whatever remains of the life he used to have when he was my age, younger. His father still lives in that city, so I can meet my other grandfather, too.

"And after that," he's said, "we'll drive to my mother's. You'll meet both your grandparents. You'll see where you came from—the other half of you."

The shingles are not gone when I leave, but there have been no more blisters for a week, and most of the old ones are now scabs. I can turn my head a little, and although my right arm is too weak to lift my backpack, I can use the fingers of that hand for short periods. "Long enough to write a postcard," I say to my mother, wiggling them.

At the airport we say good-bye with the stiff formal

kiss we always use. I feel the dry brush of her lips on my forehead, smell the faint gust of Guerlain.

"Why don't you ride with Dad?" my father says to me.

We've done all the things he said we would, and now we've come to meet his father after work. In the parking lot outside my grandfather's office, I remember three things my father has told me about his father: First, that he was so handsome in his youth, so sexually magnetic, that women he didn't know followed him down the street. Tagging along and watching the women watch his father, my father once ran into a parking meter and knocked himself out. Second, that years ago his father shot a man in his yard—a Peeping Tom who was looking at his wife. And, third, that his father was now slowly dying of prostate cancer because he has refused radiation, hormone therapy, chemotherapy, and the last-ditch removal of his testicles. So this is the way my father understands his father, and thus his own manhood: mythic sexual appeal, violent sexual jealousy, fatal sexual vanity. If only this was how I understood it at the time; but to me the stories seem quaintly exotic, their danger like that of a great white hunter who long ago put his rifle away: they seem as if they have nothing to do with me.

My grandfather, in fact, comes across as docile and friendly. He lacks the loud, large bluster of my father, but then, he is much older, his hair completely white, his walk stiff. In his car, away from the notice of my father, his hand strays past the gearshift and onto my thigh. "Oh, oh, oh," he says. "You make me wish I was thirty years younger. If I was, you'd be in trouble."

I don't dare look at him, nor pointedly away, so I stare forward out the windshield. The next time he has to change gears, he takes his hand off my leg.

My grandfather's house is small, the sidewalk before the gate cracked into big slabs heaved up by the roots of old trees. Inside is his ex-wife—his fourth ex-wife, or his third, I never get it straight. Apparently, two of the four or five marriages were to my father's mother. The ex-wife is a blowsy woman in her sixties, "mutton dressed as lamb" is how my grandmother would describe her, with her hair piled up in high curls and her wide hips packed into a tight black skirt. She still shares my grandfather's home with him; and she carries a tray of iced tea into the backyard, where my grandfather takes us on a tour of his greenhouse, devoted to the cultivation of orchids. The small glass structure is filled with color, as if every hue in this dry, gray city has been drawn into the vibrant box. In it, my grandfather is a magician, and his smile tells me he knows this. As I walk behind him and watch his hands gently turn a beautiful bloom toward my notice, do I remember the linguistic connection between orchids and male genitalia? Do I say the word silently to myself, *orchidectomy,* and define it as a surgical term for the removal of the testicles? I think, actually, that I do.

"Did you like him?" my father asks in the car on the way back to our motel.

"I liked the flowers," I say.

"But what about him, your grandfather?"

I turn in my seat to look at my father. "He made a pass at me," I say, and I describe the circumstances. My father betrays neither surprise nor disapproval.

"Maybe it's genetic," I say. "Do you think?" He bristles, and I begin to laugh, a spasm of black humor.

We eat in a coffee shop. At the motel, a squat sprawl of units built around a dusty courtyard, we share one room in which two twin beds are pushed together and covered with the same king-sized spread. Half asleep, I let my father kiss me the way he wants to, and I kiss him back.

Early in the quiet morning, I wake as suddenly as if I've been roused by a loud alarm, my heart pounding as I remember the heat of the kisses. What I feel is not so much guilt as dislocation. I look around the dim room in confusion, not knowing, for a moment, where I am. In the bed beside mine, my father sleeps, the air whistling faintly in his nose as he breathes.

I shower. I sit on the floor of the bathtub and let the hot water rain on me for an hour or more. My heartbeat doesn't slow. I watch the water curl down the drain, a yellow scum of soap at its edge.

There is a white desert in the state of New Mexico. Its beauty is unsettling: endless washes of something so white it looks like snow but burns the fingers. Each night, the wind pushes and sculpts the whiteness into great dunes and drifts, so that between dusk and dawn the whole face of the earth has changed. If you were to fall asleep, you'd wake in a place you'd never seen before.

We go there because my father wants to take pictures of me standing in that desert. As he sets up his camera, I kneel in the sand. Curiously, despite a strong wind, the place seems airless. I sigh and yawn as if I can't get enough oxygen. At my knees, the ground spreads out as white as a sheet. What I want, more than anything, is to close my eyes.

When the film is processed, the images are of a girl alone in a place without any horizon, earth indistinguishable from sky, no means by which to navigate. A car is in some of the shots, my father's long red convertible with its top down.

"Terrible car for a preacher," he concedes, looking at the prints. "Sends all the wrong messages."

I take the photographs from his hand. I study the girl in them carefully: her averted eyes, the way her blond hair, as long as her arms, blows across her open mouth. In such a place as this, is she free or is she lost? The photographs offer no clue.

We're taught to call the church our mother. My father, raised by his missionary grandmother while his mother worked as a secretary, must have heard this analogy from the time he was small, when his grandmother (who stood over six feet tall and whose imposing stature settled any disputes in which her pugnacious, diminutive husband found himself) gave him to God. Since he'd been entrusted to her, she must have assumed he was hers to give, and so, before my father's life was his own, it was returned to the church.

My father's grandmother told him that he would grow up and be a preacher. This woman's power over my father was such that her death did not release him from her wishes. After all, he owed her everything. But he resents his servitude, along with the castration implied by the robes he's forced to wear (he calls them skirts); and his insurrection finds a target in mothers: in mine and in my grandmother, who took away his wife and child; in the church itself, through whose wall he once put his fist; and, of course, in his own mother, with whom he always seems to be fighting over the most trivial matters.

My father and I drive many miles, even days, so that I can meet his mother, my other grandmother. She's married to her third husband, or maybe it's her fourth. (Again, I'm confused by the two marriages to my father's father.) They live outside of town, in a small tract of homes on a hill so windy that I watch as the welcome mat placed before the front door is whisked up off the porch and falls, moments later, in the backyard. Through the sliding glass door I see it hit, I see the dust come up around its edges.

My grandmother is not warm, but then my father hasn't led me to expect it of her. "How is your family?" she asks guardedly, separating her blood from mine.

Dinner is strained. My father does most of the talking. When he stops to chew, his stepfather tells jokes, each one more offensive than the last. He leans forward over his plate. "Why did the Jews wander in the desert for forty years?" he asks, fork in one fist, knife in the other.

"I don't know," I say. "Why?"

"Because somebody dropped a quarter!" He laughs, and I wonder if he's singling me and my family out for attack. But eventually he covers every creed and race.

After dessert, we sit stiffly in the living room, all of us in separate chairs, the couch left empty. We watch a crime drama on television, and then we go to bed. The wind moans and whistles around the corners of the house. It makes a wild, keening sound; and when my father comes quietly through the guest room's door, he finds me still awake. He pulls back the covers, and I move over, expecting that he will lie beside me, hold me in apology for the words of the stepfather

I know he dislikes. Imagining his shame, I feel sorry for him. But my father doesn't lie down.

Instead, he lifts the hem of my nightgown. He doesn't speak, and neither do I. Nor do I make any attempt to stay his hands. Beneath the nightgown I am wearing no underpants, and he opens my legs and puts his tongue between them.

His mother's house! His mother's house! I think the words over and over, aware that such a setting for his advance cannot be insignificant, but not understanding its meaning.

What he does feels neither good nor bad. It effects so complete a separation between mind and body that I don't know what I feel. Across this divide, deep and unbridgeable, my body responds independently from my mind. My heart, somewhere between them, plunges.

Neither of us speaks, not even one word. The scene is as silent, as dark and dreamlike as if it proceeded from a fever or a drug.

His mother's house.

He needs to do it at his mother's house. He needs the power granted by her presence, and he needs to thwart that power.

Algeciras, Spain, to Copenhagen, Denmark: thirty-seven hours. Copenhagen to Milan: twenty-nine hours. Milan to Monaco to Paris to Munich: fifty-three hours. My Eurail pass grants me unlimited train travel. Transit is narcotic, fleeing irresistible.

In Europe, I spend still more money I've begged from my grandparents, now eager to encourage me along any path that might lead me away from the father they sense looms ever larger and more dangerous.

Neither here nor there, it's not that I intentionally ponder my life back home from the safety of my train compartment, but that it unfurls like a flower on a hilltop we pass, a story in a book or on a screen. My father is more distant than the little cows and cars I rush past. The noise of the rails alternately lulls me to sleep and rattles me awake.

I don't use a youth hostel unless I have to. I exchange only as much money as I need to pay for a shower in the station's public bathhouse, a meal in the station's café. The economy of this makes me feel safe—how little I need, really, to sustain me—and it's a relief to be excused from the routine scramble of arrival: queuing up in the tourist information office, finding lodging, getting to it under my heavy pack, trudging wearily off toward sights and galleries.

On the trains, I never spend the surcharge for a berth. I just throw the pack on the shelf overhead and curl into the seat by the window. On hot days I lift the bottom pane and let the wind blow in; fierce and dry, it whips tears from my eyes. At night, if we go through cities, the lit rooms of unknown families flash by, squares of yellow light containing little people gathered around a table.

Sometimes I miscalculate. I misread the fine print of my Thomas Cook timetable digest, itself often incorrect, and the train I thought would continue terminates in a small town; or I settle into the wrong coach, and while the front end of the train goes on to my planned destination, I discover too late that I've been left behind in a car that has stopped moving.

A few times I arrive somewhere too late to get lodgings and have to sleep in the station waiting room. Once, when a station closes at 2:00 A.M., I have to spend the rest of the night outside. In a dusty, cool plaza I'm the object of interest to local tramps. If this is dangerous, I don't know it, or I don't care.

I posit lives for myself, other lives than the one to which I will return. Lives that begin when I don't return. There are always those stories of young women, they just never come home.

I talk to my father a few times. I call him collect from the stations, less often than I said I would. Each time when he answers, he is excited, then angry, and at last fretful.

"Call sooner next time," he says. "Don't make me wait so long."

"Okay," I say, "I won't." But I break my word.

"Don't let me be alone," he says. "Don't leave me all alone with my love."

Do I notice that his words express the history of my life with my mother: *Don't leave me alone with my love.* Whether or not I take pause, at last I know how it feels to be on the other side of that plea.

I return to school, as I promised my grandparents I would. My senior year, I live off campus in a house I share with four other girls. The September to June rental agreement stipulates that no more than four tenants may occupy the dwelling; legally, one of the five of us does not exist. The names on the lease do not include my own; and the house, vulnerable to surprise visits from the real estate agent, has only four bedrooms and four beds, none of which is mine. I sleep either on the couch or on the floor; and on a few chilly weekend mornings I have to slip out the back door in my nightgown and wait in the shrubs while the suspicious agent either inspects the house or shows it to prospective buyers. It's a surpassingly pleasant and leafy neighborhood in which we live, the house itself an emblem of middle-American comfort and normalcy, and this is undoubtedly why I can't take my place in it.

My father withdraws his outsized Mont Blanc fountain pen from the pocket inside his jacket. It's among the phallic possessions that he most esteems. He pushes our untouched plates of food aside and places one of his business cards on the table. He hands me the pen, its barrel still warm from the heat of his flesh.

"Draw two intersecting circles," he says. "One to represent you and the other to represent me. The area of intersection will show how closely you feel we should live our lives. The place we connect. The extent to which commitment joins us." He folds his arms.

I take the pen. My picture looks like one of the eights I made as a child, before I could do it without lifting the pencil from the paper: the two circles overlap, but not by much. He nods, takes the pen. His picture looks like one circle drawn twice, the lines almost superimposed.

I look at the pictures and my heart pounds with a sudden wild insistence. What I said is true, then. I thought I was being dramatic, but he does want it all, the whole of my life. He wants to leave only the little soap-bubble skin of the circle for me. The scruff of my neck, perhaps, the callus on my heel.

I'm afraid you may be frightened by this admission, one letter's postscript reads, *but I have ruined an entire box of envelopes substituting your address for mine and mine for yours.*

I'm not as frightened as I should be. I don't see that the destruction of his internal boundaries will of necessity erode my own. Nor do I shudder, as I will years later, when I read missives addressed to *Beatrice,* my father's pet name for me, whom he beseeches to guide him on the journey down through the dark circles of his soul, just as Dante's beloved in the *Divine Comedy* revealed to the poet what for so long had been hidden. Inside my father, his letters confess, are *emptiness, wastelands,* and *black holes* that only my love can fill.

For nearly forty years, he writes, *I've worked to create the man I've become. What or who lies beneath the surface of all my accomplishments I do not know. You are my only hope of discovering myself.* My eyes move over such words without understanding them. I don't allow myself to hear my father confess that he lacks identity.

He calls as many as three times a day. "How am I?" he says when he calls, and he says he says this because how he is depends utterly on how much I love him. Without me, there is no meaning, purpose, or pleasure in his life.

As a child, did I frighten my mother the way my father frightens me? When I stood by her bed waiting for her to wake—to give me to myself—she was the same age that I am now. So even as I take my father from her, I learn what it was to *be* her: to be so young and vulnerable, to have to protect herself from a ravenous love that she was afraid would consume her, steal her from herself.

In the car, my father pleads and threatens. I've admitted that I still correspond with my old boyfriend, now two thousand miles away. The angrier my father gets, the louder he yells, the further I retreat into silence. It's not a strategy but a reflex, something left over from my mother's anger, the French drills. I hear his strident tones, and I fall into what seems like a stupor. Inside, I feel as if I've shrunk, my essence distilled into a safe, impermeable core far within my body, far below its surface. I form answers to his accusations but cannot move my lips to speak them. Mile markers flash by; in the car I'm propelled along the weary trajectory of both his anger and the road, no end in sight.

"Is it possible that you don't realize my devotion? You say I'm disrupting your studies, but don't you see that you've wreaked havoc in my heart! Only you matter to me!"

Again and again, we return to the "expression of love." He must possess me physically, for only that will reassure him of my commitment to him. Nothing else will suffice. Nothing less. Does he mean that without such reassurance, he'll stop loving me? I don't ask.

The whole visit, it seems, is awash with tears, his and mine. The exhaustion of withstanding his desire is not supportable.

When I give up, it's almost a relief, the way it must be for someone who, holding tight to a ledge, at last lets go. After the agony of resistance, when for so long it's been clear that a fall is imminent, plummeting is a kind of fulfillment. I plunge without knowing how fast I fall or how far, how hard the bottom will be when I hit.

Five, ten, fifteen years later, the only thing I can remember is my father's undressing and my shock at discovering that he's uncircumcised. Raised in a Jewish household, I've never before seen such a thing, I can't help but find it alien, unclean.

The sight of him naked: at that point I fall completely asleep. I arrive at the state promised by the narcotic kiss in the airport. In years to come, I won't be able to remember even one instance of our lying together. I'll have a composite, generic memory. I'll know that he was always on top and that I always lay still, as still as if I had, in truth, fallen from a great height. I'll remember such details as the color of the carpet in a particular motel room, or the kind of tree outside the window. That he always wore his socks and that I wore whatever I could. I'll remember every tiny thing about him. I will be able to close my eyes and see the pattern of hair that grew on the backs of his hands, the mole on his cheek, the lines, each one of them, at the corners of his eyes. But I won't be able to remember what it felt like. No matter how hard I try, pushing myself to inhabit my past, I'll recoil from what will always seem impossible.

Asleep. There's the cottony somnolence of my days. There's the little trick of selective self-anesthesia that leaves me awake to certain things and dead to others. There are drugs and alcohol, and there is food, too much or too little, with which to bludgeon the senses. Over time I make use of each of these, and perhaps others of which I am still not aware.

Sleep in response to unbearable desire: I have learned this from my mother. My psychic sleep is often not distinguishable from real sleep. My father calls me on the phone. I answer, and after the first few minutes of conversation, I drop off. I don't mean to, but still, it makes him wild with anger. What evasion could be more absolute? When I wake, often as much as an hour after he has hung up in frustration, the phone, still off the hook, is bleating in my ear. No strategy works to control this. I tell myself I'll stand throughout the conversation. At the first prickle of fatigue I bite my fingertips or the skin on the backs of my hands. Black coffee, No-Doz, amphetamines: nothing can prevent this sleep. As if under an enchantment, I sink inevitably to the floor. My housemates walk over or around my body, itself curled around the receiver. If they need to use the phone, they take it from my hand.

I sleep not because of the shock of my father's lust—at least not shock in the sense of something sudden and surprising. I have known what he wants from the start. And yet I am shocked, as I have been from my first sight of him, when he turned from the drinking fountain, his mouth wet, dripping. So yes, I sleep because I'm shocked, and because I'm frightened. I want to avoid contemplating the enormity of what we're doing—an act that defines me, that explains who I am, because in it is all the hurt and anger and hunger of my past, and in it, too, is the future.

It's anger that frightens me most. I sleep to escape my rage. Not at him, but at my mother. To avoid owning a fury so destructive that I would take from her what brief love she has known, because she has been so unwilling for so long to love me just a little.

The other object of my anger is myself. The good girl who failed, the thin girl, the achiever, the grade-earner, the quiet girl, the unhungry girl, the girl who will shape-shift and perform any self-alchemy to win her mother's love. She failed, and I must destroy her. Obliterate this good daughter with one so bad that what she does is unspeakable.

At the same time, I can, of course, make myself the sacrifice my father's love demands. One single act to destroy my old master and to serve my new one.

But I don't want to contemplate this.

I prefer to sleep.

We have never been closer than we are now, my mother and I.

Guilt makes me draw near to her, and I go home to visit whenever I can, days that teach me there is an almost sickening intimacy between the betrayer and the person betrayed. Through my father I have begun at last to penetrate my mother, to tear away the masks that divide us. And now, even as I draw closer to her to judge the level of her suspicions, she comes closer to me to monitor what she fears.

In her house, my heart pounds, my hands shake. The smell of her perfume, the glint of sun on her hair, the way that, in her small kitchen, our bodies sometimes inadvertently touch, separated by no more than the fabric of two thin nightgowns: any of these is enough to make me feel faint.

My mother and I are gentle, polite, and careful with each other, as careful as only enemies need be. We don't speak about him, we watch each other across the dining table. As if afraid that she might poison me, I pick at the food she cooks. Whatever I swallow, I throw up.

On one of my visits home, I get what I've waited for: her accusation. She takes me to her psychiatrist's office, the little brown room where she talks about her mother. Though she doesn't tell me the agenda of the session—"just to talk"—I must suspect what will unfold, because I wear something so uncharacteristic that it still fills me with wonder. It's a dress I bought and then hid in a closet at my grandparents' without taking it out of the bag. So short I can't bend over without my underpants showing, it's made out of a pale purple stretch velour that hugs my body tightly. For our appointment, I wear it with high heels.

When my mother picks me up at my grandparents', she says nothing, but her eyes widen; her cheeks look pink, as if slapped. It's the first time she's seen me in something that isn't long and black and baggy.

Just walking into her doctor's office, sitting on the coffee-colored couch, I sense my mother's doom there in the dead brown color of the walls, in the way her doctor's hand perspires, even in his skinny, dotted-

Swiss necktie. She'll never escape her mother; she'll never stop hearing the screams from behind the bedroom door. My grandmother has her in a death grip. Is this because my mother is not as ruthless as I am?

She gets to the point without preamble. "I think they're having sex," she says.

The doctor turns to me, his eyebrows raised, and I lie as I have never lied before or since. I'm a bad liar, generally, but on this afternoon, wearing what I'm wearing, I am brilliant.

"It just looks bad," I tell him. "I know why she's worried. But . . . it's just that . . ." I falter. "See, I never knew my father. I'm going through a stage, like all little girls, just later than most."

I pause at exactly the right moments. My performance is so good that I'm frightened. Is my personality so unformed that putting on a dress is enough to change it? Or is this shameless, sexual, purple-clad girl—someone I can't imagine as a friend—a part of me? "She's right," I say, nodding. "I am in love with him, but it . . . I'm not . . . I'd never . . . I wouldn't do that."

The doctor looks at me sitting before him in my vulgar dress, and he believes me. I know it, and so does my mother. He's mine, not hers, and so I have what I wanted—what I thought I wanted. She is alone. I've taken her husband and now her only ally, the one person with whom she can share her troubles.

And I, I begin to know the misery of wounding the person I love most. Seeing her face as she watches me speak, watching the death of any hope that was there, not just my heart but my whole body throbs in sympathy.

When we get home, I throw the dress out. I run down the driveway at my grandparents' house and throw it in the garbage. Later, I go outside with scissors. I stand in the dark and I cut the dress up. Head bent over the garbage can, I expect to weep, but don't. Instead, I find myself moaning, making a noise that, if I didn't know it came from me—if I were inside and heard it rising out of the night—I'd think it was an animal, something dying in the road.

Student Health offers ten free hours of therapy, and the psychologist to whom I'm assigned is young and earnest. His hair is cut very short as if to display his balding head as honestly as possible. His eyes crinkle in lines as evocative of tears as of laughter.

"Well," he says, sometime during my second visit. He puts a box of tissues in my lap. "I understand that something is wrong. You're upset, obviously. But I can't really help you if you won't talk to me."

I nod, tears washing from my face down my neck.

"So," he says. "It's fine for you to come back. But perhaps you'd like to wait a couple of weeks? Maybe it would be better for you to come back when you feel like you can talk."

I nod. I don't come back.

How can I say what I need to say to this decent young man with his decent scant brown hair, his cheerful bow tie, the squeaky-clean vision imparted by his tortoiseshell glasses?

We spend our nights in motels not so much sordid as depressing. Sordid has a style and swagger these places lack, rooms with curtains cut from the same orange fabric as the bedspread, ceilings of plaster textured like cottage cheese. The paint on the wall around the vents is gray, a pattern that betrays in which direction the air flows, air stained by the smoke of long-extinguished cigarettes.

We drive to Lake Havasu, near Arizona's western

border, where the original London Bridge has been reassembled over a man-made stream in the desert. On the underside of the span, numbers have been inscribed on the stones; they indicate the order in which the structure was dismantled and then put back together. At either end of this historic crossing that now goes from nowhere to nowhere is a tiny fake Tudor village with fish-and-chip stands and racks of Union Jack postcards.

We walk back and forth across the bridge's cobbled road. The desert sun burns our heads. "No fog," he says, and I laugh. It's hysteria, not mirth. For me, raised in a Victorian British household in which we had high tea every day at four, the London Bridge torn down and rebuilt in the Mojave Desert is the logical end of the earth.

Later, at dinner, we begin once again to argue about my father's need to control me. We fight over any independence I exhibit, whether of body, of mood, of thought. We fight over the clothes I wear and whether they might show any other man a snatch of the flesh my father considers his own. We fight over whether *Paradise Lost* is the greatest work ever written and whether its completion was worth the enslavement of the blind poet's daughters. We fight about my unwillingness to fight, about whether my silences are a hostile strategy or simply bewildered exhaustion.

My father leans across the table. His face is the same shape but much larger than mine, seemingly larger than other men's. At close range, it seems planetary. "You," he says, too loudly for a restaurant, "are a slut just like your mother."

Everyone who hears turns to see who the big man is talking to with such righteous conviction. My father has a knife in his hand. He lays it down on the table. I feel my face burn with shame, and consider, for a moment, running outside. But the gesture would be just that: a gesture. I have no money with me. My father would chase me over the bridge or down to the lake's stagnant green banks. He'd cry, of course, and so would I. These scenes of recrimination and apology, they cost so much energy, and nothing is accomplished by them.

I put my face in my hands; I block it from the eyes of all the people who think they're looking at a slut.

My father's tears. Like the eyes from which they flow, they change everything. His crying convinces me he has no control over what he does or what he demands of me. His actions seem helpless in a way I never understand my mother's to be. To her I have always, and undoubtedly unfairly, accorded a volition that I and my father now lack. Is this because of her inability to weep? My mother has always been frozen against her tears, dry-eyed in misery.

Unused as I am to ready grief, I allow my father's tears to excuse anything. All his aggressive apparatuses—pistols, shotguns, cameras, cars, fountain pens—and his weeping while aiming them at life, at me; the way the tears drip down his face and onto my chest when he is over me: his tears afford him my forgiveness.

My enslavement to my father blights the last summer my mother, my grandparents, and I spend together at the shore. There's no privacy in our rundown cottage, the place we've rented each summer for all of my life. In order to call my father, I have to use the public telephone in the nearby park. I make myself as small as possible in the dank booth. Wet Kleenex squelches underfoot, sand in the receiver abrades my chin, and the connection is poor, hissing with static. Everything seems designed to torment me as I look nervously through the dull, greasy glass to see if my grandfather is coming down the hill, or if my mother is peering out of the cottage window, trying to catch me.

"I can't stand this," my father says. "I can't take any more. I have to see you."

Nothing satisfies him, not a nightly call, not a twice-daily call. It becomes increasingly difficult to steal away from every occasion, every evening. My family says nothing, but they know where I'm going, they know that if I were calling a boyfriend I wouldn't have to sneak away.

Each time I return from one of my lonely errands, everyone looks up in silence. The old wooden screen door sighs shut behind me. My grandfather presses the mute button on the television's remote control, interrupting the news to give me an opportunity to explain myself. My grandmother puts down her magazine, and my mother replaces the tiny brush in her bottle of nail polish.

Sometimes I make the obligatory meaningless comment. "The tide's up," I say. Or, having taken the long way home, past the market or the bakery, I hold up a bag of pastries for breakfast. I move through the cramped living room with my face averted, not allowing any eye contact. My grandfather turns the television's sound back on. My grandmother returns to her magazine article, my mother to her nails. In the kitchen, I quietly open the door of the bread box and place my purchase inside.

It was in this yellow kitchen that, when I was fifteen, I blew up the old gas oven. My grandmother, checking to see if the pilot light had for once remained ignited, turned the knob to *high* and peered inside: no flame. As usual, it would have to be lit by hand. She turned the knob back in the direction of *off,* but not all the way, allowing gas to seep from the jets into the closed oven, where we couldn't smell it.

"Light the pilot, will you?" she said a few minutes later, a request made to either my mother or me, both of us just back from the beach and rummaging in the cupboards. I took the box of Blue Diamond matches from where it stood between the salt and pepper shakers on the little shelf over the stove.

I liked using the big wooden kitchen matches. I opened the oven door partway, leaned into it and struck one, in a gesture of adolescent affectation, against the sole of my sandal. The oven door blew open the rest of the way, hitting my shins, and the stove's burner pans leapt up in sympathy. There was an enormous rush of air, as if the house itself had gasped. The room was filled with flames.

No one spoke. My grandmother, my mother, and I all turned to its center and to one another, as if participating in a bizarre rite. We gasped, too, echoing the house. A web of fire hung between us. Tongues of it licked at everything: the curtains, our clothing, our hair. I saw flames in the lenses of my grandmother's eyeglasses. And then they were gone, it was over. We fell into one another's arms, weeping with fright, laughing in relief. When we pulled apart we saw how, among us, only I, closest to the oven, had lost my eyelashes and eyebrows, the hair on my arms and legs, and the outermost layer of the hair on my head. A fine white dusting of ash coated me. It fell from my limbs as I moved.

"Oh God," we said, over and over. "Oh God."

My grandfather came to the door. "What's happened?" he said. "What on earth has happened in here?"

We didn't answer. We wept and laughed and touched one another's faces.

. . .

At the shore, my mother and I walk along the breakwater. Curved into the ocean like an eyelash, its old railing is so rusty that in places it crumbles at our touch and leaves stains like those of blood on our hands. We look into the water below and say little to each other, flat in our separate torment, betrayer and betrayed. The sand scratches and sighs between our shoes and the walkway. The wind is hard, our faces are wet with spray, and we move slowly along the narrow path, not lifting our feet but sliding them forward like old ladies. White foam covers the cracked paving at our feet.

"See how strong the water is," my mother says at last. "Someday it will knock all these stones down."

It frightens me to stand on the breakwater with my mother. I imagine myself stumbling, falling, a victim of my own gravity, of my desire for oblivion, for release from feeling. Because I feel too much—I always have—and it's impossible to live with my heart always breaking, equally impossible to keep myself anesthetized. If I were to die in a fall from the breakwater, the last thing I'd smell would be the seaweed rotting on the beach. The last thing I'd see would be my mother's face, like that of a clock: still, flat, and white, marked with the hour of my death.

All summer, I am never warm; the sun can't touch me. I go for long, solitary swims, frequenting dangerous beaches unattended by lifeguards. I go in bad weather, rain sizzling and hissing on the sand, and I go at dusk as the light fades and glitters on the sea. I swim underwater, eyes closed, for as many strokes as I can. If the tide is low, kelp tangles around my legs, shells and pebbles move with the ebb and flow of the water. They make a sound like hundreds of teeth coming together, chewing and grinding.

One night I swim out to one of the buoys that mark the boundaries of the oceanographic institute's preserve, three-quarters of a mile away from the shore. When I reach the buoy, I try to grab onto the algae-slick sides of the big, bobbing metal ball, but it offers no handhold. The swells are so large that they obscure the lights of the town that glimmer from the shore.

The greatest danger of swimming in the dark is that one can swim for some time, turned around by the riptide and heading out to sea without knowing it. I'm so cold on the way back that I cut my legs on rocks and coral without feeling it, so cold that hours in a hot bath cannot stop my teeth from chattering.

Nights, in my room, I turn the handle of my grandfather's old-fashioned razor to release the blade from under its stainless steel cover. I trace the sharp edge over my arm, press it into places where a scratch might go unnoticed. It's not so much a desire for punishment as for manageable pain, bleeding that can be stanched.

I give my mother every opportunity to accuse me again—alone, just the two of us—but she takes none. We watch each other.

I don't go to graduate school. Instead, I move to New York, the city where I naively imagine writers must go. My portion of the rent for the apartment I share with two other women is five hundred dollars a month. It's on Henry Street, in Brooklyn Heights, and would be small for a single occupant. We decide to make a loft in the back room in order to fit all the beds inside it and leave the front room free for living space. The luck of the draw is such that I get the uppermost bed, over which the ceiling is so low that I can't sit up at night to read, the only way I know to fall asleep.

I told my family I was moving east to become a writer, but how am I to begin? My savings and the two thousand dollars my grandparents gave me seem like very little between me and the world. Every day, I go to the public library and work in notebooks or on index cards on my postmodern novel, in which an existential hero sets out for where I'm not sure and against what I don't know. The story's essence is loneliness and disorientation. The hero's companion is a monkey—undoubtedly because of all creatures they seem so like people, and yet can't speak. Because my father has at last separated me from the rest of the world and I can no longer imagine human friendship.

My days are as long as despair can make them. I begin taking endless and exhausting walks to nowhere, just block after block into Brooklyn or over the bridge into Manhattan. Outside a seedy-looking beauty salon in Chinatown, a little man with long black mustaches offers me three hundred dollars for my hair. I gather the long mass of it into my hands. "No," I say. "Okay, five," he says. I shake my head, keep walking, holding so tightly to the hank of hair that my hand sweats.

I spend hours of each day sitting on a bench on the promenade, looking at the bridges over the East River, sometimes turning to consider the houses behind me, wondering in which Norman Mailer lives, if he still lives there, and if that's the place where he stabbed his wife, if she was his wife. Or maybe he just waved a knife at her, whoever she was.

The only thing that provides any structure to my time are the calls from my father, and his letters, their content always the same: he loves me, separation is torture. Having waited for the mail to arrive, I sometimes find myself unable to open the envelopes, to read the messages they contain.

. . . *I gave you my flesh and blood, my spirit. It is my heart that beats within you. I have as much right to you as any one, as much as you have to yourself* . . .

Early in the morning, late at night, at home, in a library: my father's words of what he calls love retain their narcotic effect in any setting, under any circumstance. Years later I'll go back to the letters, 839 pages, all saved in a locked chest. Determined to get through them, I'll pack a suitcase full and take them on a plane to a distant city. In my hotel room I'll order a large pot of coffee, and after swallowing three tablets of No-Doz, I'll spread the letters over the bed and the desk and the dresser. As I stack them chronologically by month, I'll note with surprise how many were abandoned on first reading, replaced in the envelope after I had gotten no further than page two of the five or more sheets it contained.

I'll drink all the coffee, open the windows for cold, fresh air, and then I'll curl up on the floor and sleep for five hours. When I wake, the room will be frigid and wind will have scattered the pages I can't read. I'll return home with them disordered and crammed any which way into the suitcase, having yet again avoided my father's telling me, *You are all of life to me, and I must be the same for you. . . . You accuse me of being a jailer; you must learn the definition of freedom. . . .*

You ask me to be a father to you. I will define what it is to be a father.

I lose my appetite. I have a cough. My days are filled with my obsession: whether to see him, when to see him, when not to see him. Like a more prosaic addiction—to alcohol, to heroin—mine for my father has consumed the rest of my life. I take no pleasure in its satisfaction, and yet I cannot see beyond it, *him,* to anything else, even myself.

I spend a lot of time in neighborhood boutiques, trying on clothes I have no intention of buying, looking at myself in dressing-room mirrors. I've always been drawn to mirrors, not out of vanity but for reassurance. I want to see that I'm there, and I don't resist any reflective surface—puddles, shop windows, the sides of the tea kettle.

It's a habit left over from childhood, my mother's

sleep mask. To believe in myself I'd leave her bedside and look in the mirror on her closet door. I'd stand before the image of myself for whole minutes, just to make sure that I was real and not a trick of the light, a phantom that might evaporate like the steam that roiled out from under the curtain when at last she got up and showered.

Even now, in the stores, I don't look at the clothes but at the pale face above them. Now, I no longer know who I am, or *if* I am, apart from my father.

He stays in a nearby hotel, one within walking distance of my apartment. I make the reservation by phone and draw no conclusions from the fact that the rooms are available on only a weekly basis. My father, when he arrives, is shocked by the accommodations. And I'm surprised as well, but there's a difference: I think it's terribly funny that he is staying in a welfare hotel, that this is the environment in which he will ravish me. I feel that in my own story I've at last arrived in the dirty place I belong. As for my father's squeamishness, it strikes me as something he cannot afford, morally.

The lobby of the hotel is carpeted in red, as if to

allow for a more discreet spilling of blood. The walls are white (or they were), the man behind the desk black, his teeth gold. Upstairs, the halls teem with life of all description: winos, cockroaches, junkies. I sit on the bed in my father's room only after checking the sheets, which are, in fact, clean. When I pull off the spread, Clorox fumes rise from beneath it.

He wants to take pictures. *Naked ones,* I call them, as opposed to the word on which he insists: nudes. But *nude* implies art, and without my clothes the photographs my father makes of me have the same quality as those documenting medical anomalies.

"I'll show you who you are," he said to me when he took the first pictures. In these latest images the expression on my face, flat and dispossessed, is one I see years later in a museum exhibit of pictures taken of soldiers injured during the Civil War. Undressed and propped against walls or on crutches, the veterans reveal those places where bullets entered and, perhaps, exited.

My father strings a little wire from one side of the room to another, a line on which to hang his wet Polaroids. I sit on the bed and laugh, still in response to his outrage over the hotel. I can't stop laughing. Hysterics, perhaps, because I'm crying at the same time.

"It's just that—" I gasp, trying to explain, but it's no use. Perhaps my father laughs only in social adaptation at what other people find amusing. When he does, the noise he makes is not quite right. It's off, the way a deaf person's speech never sounds like that of someone who can hear.

It's in this room, a few days later, that I capitulate. All right, I say. I'll give it a try. My father has offered to support me for a year while I write. I'll live in his home, use an office at his church. After all, I have nowhere else to go. My father stands between me and the rest of life, my family, the friends I once had.

In keeping with the whole of our affair, everything about this plan seems both wrong and inevitable. From the start, we've had to meet in rooms such as the one we're in, rooms for addicts and prostitutes, people who exist outside the social contract. Does my father believe that he can take me home to his wife and children, whom I've met on only a few awkward occasions? That the two of us can live in the midst of other people? I don't ask these questions. I have no life or will apart from his.

. . .

I drive west without making an overnight stop. It cannot be true, but it seems that the road is perpetually wet, the sun always in my eyes, the wind and every natural force against me.

At about 3:00 AM, just outside Oklahoma's Oral Roberts University in Tulsa, I come upon the four-hundred-foot-tall cutout of Jesus in His purple robe and crown, rising over the highway with supernatural luminosity. Trucks scream past me in the black night. How long is it since I've slept or eaten? I'm afraid, more than I like to admit, that I'm seeing things.

Ten miles beyond the billboard Jesus, a grass fire is burning, and no one stops it. I pull the car over to the side of the road and get out. The ground under my feet is black. The fire advances, a red line no more than thirty yards from where I stand. I sit on the hood of my car to watch its progress.

Truckers blow their horns as they pass me. They call out lewd remarks.

When I can't see the fire anymore, I get back in the car, I drive to catch up with it, stop, get out again. I go on like this until dawn, when the sun comes up and makes the narrow line of flame invisible.

A new carpet on the linoleum floor and a print of one of my favorite paintings over the bed can't disguise the fact that in my father's house I am to sleep and dress in a room without privacy, one separated from the kitchen by no more than an open-slatted wooden door, nor that this room offers the only access to the backyard where the children play.

My place within this home proves to be like that of a young aunt or old child—someone taken in for a spell while she gets her bearings or her footing or whatever it might be that she needs to equip her for independent life. At least this is the announced reason for my father's insisting on bringing me under his roof. Just as the parsonage itself is so prototypically middle-American that it evokes the opening credits of a situation comedy, so does my father's wife bear the same pleasant, harried, slightly madcap expression as a television mother, although her smile doesn't hide the fact that she is as frightened of me as I am of her.

She tolerates my presence because she is as controlled by my father as I am, and because she seems to consider me a project that might be saved by Christian guidance and clean living. At some point, she alludes to the promiscuous college life I used to lead, and I gather that my father has portrayed me as a girl who has gone awry as a result of my grandparents' and mother's permissiveness.

In this house I am afforded an intimate look at the kind of family for which I've always longed: parents who are still married to each other, a father who has a demanding and admirable job, and a mother who raises children, shops, cooks, cleans, and teaches Bible school. Everyone attends church on Sunday; the children go to Little League games and Girl Scout troop meetings; they come home from school to homework, chores, and piano practice. Picture perfect, and yet sitting next to my father at the dinner table and knowing what relation I bear to the head of this family, how can I not question all of what I otherwise might assume was happiness?

Initially, everything, including my sudden appearance at my father's church, proceeds with unnerving smoothness, a testimony to my father's absolute control over his family and his staff. Even his younger children, otherwise garrulous, do not betray that I am the shadow daughter from an unacknowledged, failed marriage. After the eleven o'clock service, a number of people in the informal receiving line at the door comment on how young my father's wife appears. Can she possibly have so grown-up a daughter as I? Following one of these remarks, my father's wife looks at me, and then we both look away.

"Do they think I'm—" I ask later, hesitating. My father and I are alone in the office of his church; I'm sitting in the big leather chair from which he used to call me after his staff had gone home.

"They think you're her eldest, too," he says.

"Your wife's, you mean? From the same marriage as your other children."

"Yes."

I nod, say nothing. But I am surprised, and stung, at how easily my mother and grandparents and the past two decades—all of my life up until the point at which he reentered it—have been erased. Cut out of the picture, leaving even less than my grandmother's nail scissors.

"The bishop and the board know you're not," he says, as if reading my thoughts. "But no one thought there was any reason to announce it to the church as a whole."

"I see." I look at the surface of his desk: the immaculate blotter, the ordered stacks of correspondence, the glass bottle of ink and the clutch of fountain pens. The awful simplicity and tidiness of the lie—the same as his condescending sermon that delivered all the certainty of faith, and none of its doubts, its pain.

My father's possessing me physically seems increasingly to be just that: Each time, he takes a little more of my life; each time, there is less of me left.

He drives us to his church, the place where he has long waited to do this. He unlocks the little office he's given me for my work, and he takes me on the floor by the desk. Following his lead in imposing a religious context on the act, I concentrate on mortification of the flesh. I tell myself that if I give myself over to him to be sullied, then by the topsy-turvy Christian logic that exalts the reviled, I'll be made clean. I will if I can just do it willingly, trusting in the ultimate goodness of God, and the way in which he sometimes takes unexpected and even repugnant forms, like beggars and lepers, like Saint Dymphna's father. How could she have been martyred without him? How could she have been glorified?

The heat of our early kisses was lost long ago on the highways; the weight of him has smothered the passion I once felt; and the workaday drudgery of our contact flattens me to the point that each time I am more still, more silent, more lifeless. We fight about this. "I hate it that you tolerate me!" my father yells, and I put my face in my hands, I cover my eyes. "What do you think that does to me! How do you think it makes me feel!"

I'm sick. My cough gets worse, and one morning I find I have a high fever, I'm too weak to sit up in bed. My father's wife has to help me to get dressed.

I have pneumonia, news that I regard with some interest and relief. Please, please let it be fatal, I pray silently. Or at least serious enough that my fate is placed in the care of competent, impersonal professionals.

"I'm sure you'll be fine," the doctor says. He asks

my father to leave the room for a moment. My father has accompanied me into the examining room, watched as the doctor thumped my ribs and stood between us as the doctor asked me to remove my bra. "She'll be with you soon," the doctor says to him.

"Do I have to go to the hospital?" I ask.

"No," he says. He looks at me, my tears dripping onto my paper kimono. The chest X rays hang behind his head, my narrow bones luminous in their ghostly envelope of flesh, my heart a tipped shadow among the rooting bronchi.

"Is there something you'd like to tell me?" the doctor asks.

I shake my head.

He sighs. "Well," he says. "Maybe you'll come to the next appointment by yourself," he suggests. "Maybe you'll be feeling much better and your father won't have to drive you."

Despite hourly prayers for deterioration, a steadfast refusal of food, and throwing up the antibiotics, I do get better. Twice a day I have to lie belly-down on the bed, my head as close to the floor as I can get it, and be whacked on the back by my father's wife while I choke up phlegm into a bowl. This seemingly anachronistic element of my program of recovery, its evocation of a tubercular, Dickensian slum, strikes me as appropriately punitive, especially at the hands of my father's wife. Like a small child, my fantasies during the procedure are those of my own funeral, at which my mother and my father weep inconsolably.

My mother has fallen ill, as well. But her treatments are state-of-the-art, so modern they seem futuristic. One day, while reading the newspaper, her fingers splayed thoughtlessly on her chest as she leans over the arts page spread on the breakfast table, my mother discovers a lump in her left breast, a little one, quite palpable and hard. It's excised and found to be malignant, and a margin of tissue surrounding it is taken as well: all in all, about an egg-sized subtraction.

She doesn't tell me until it's done, and by the time I fly from my father's to see her, she's back in the hospital undergoing postoperative therapy. She opens her gown to show me her breast, and the position of her hands around the sutured rent in her flesh reminds me of the familiar image of Christ displaying His bleeding heart.

The freshly livid scar is made incidental by the

radium implants that are supposed to wipe out stray cancer cells. "Sputniks" are what we call the implants, because they look like space probes. Two long stainless-steel skewers disappear into the white skin around her nipple, their ends bearing tiny, complex apparatuses.

Everyone is afraid to touch the sputniks, not just my mother and I, but also the hospital personnel. A securely lidded can outside her room's private bathroom is marked HAZARDOUS WASTE. DEPARTMENT OF NUCLEAR MEDICINE, and the younger nurses won't come in because they're afraid that radioactive contaminants will leak out of my mother and cost them their fertility. They make a wide swath around the door to her room.

"Does it hurt?" I ask.

"Not really," she says, her head cocked quizzically on one side, her eyes on mine as if to ask how much her pain might concern me.

I cannot account for the days, nor the weeks, nor the months. They are all the same and all of them lost. Not forgotten, because they were never lived.

I read many books, walk many blocks, write a few

stories, and then rewrite them. Every day is a drowning. Except for brief spasms of weeping that leave my face as wet as if I actually have, for a moment, broken the surface of some frigid dark lake, I feel nothing.

My self-anesthesia may be involuntary, but it is not easy or idle. For the first time in my life I slide into serious bulimia, the business of consuming and rejecting food useful for the hours it wastes. I never understand it for what it is: a painful parody of hunger and the satisfaction of hunger with something that demands my being sick, a secret ritual of appetite and addiction. I never taste what I eat. Sometimes I don't even know what it is until I've thrown it up.

I consider going to the bishop, but I'm afraid of losing my father his job. Haven't I wronged his family enough? It's not his wife that I worry about. After all, she knows that it happens, she lets him do it. All she asks, my father tells me, is that he be considerate enough to spare her any evidence of his affair with his daughter. She and I deserve each other, both of us too weak to deny my father his impossible demands. But what of their children? Their eldest daughter is a girl I've come to love, and who seems genuinely to love me, even though my arrival has cost her so much. Deposed as oldest child and favorite daughter, she starts spending more and more time at her school's gymnasium. She outweighs me and she has big muscles.

"I could beat you up," she says, flexing her biceps under my nose so that I can admire them. "I could really clean your clock."

"Definitely," I agree. I wish she would black my eyes and bloody my nose, but what I get instead is a sweet peal of laughter, bravado, the inevitable kiss. Does she know why it is that I cry when she embraces me? How I wish that I were her, sinned against, not sinning? Both jealous and appalled, she does not name but recognizes my plight. Years younger than I, she holds me in her arms. Perhaps she thinks I've saved her from my fate.

When my half sister and I meet again, it's in another city, miles away, years later. She sends letter after letter to my publisher until at last I reply. There is a debt I owe her, one I can't repay, but I know it would be unkind and cowardly to refuse to see her.

According to plans made awkwardly over the phone, we meet in the train station of a city between our homes and go from there to a restaurant in a nearby mall. We have barely two hours to catch up on a decade.

"I'm sorry," I say. It's something I've never said in person.

"It's okay," she says. "Me too."

She's pregnant by her second husband, and I bring her a bag of maternity clothes I no longer need. She tells me that she fled her parents' home at eighteen, the age at which she always promised that she'd go. Her first husband was a soldier trained in hand-to-hand combat, who used his special skills on her. To escape him, she returned briefly to our father's house with her cat, the pet with which she slept when she managed to lock her husband out of the bedroom.

By this time my father had left the church; he occupied part of his time with the breeding of attack dogs. The dogs killed his daughter's cat.

"The poor little thing went over the fence into their pen and they just ripped her up," my half sister says, dry-eyed, smiling her wry smile.

"Oh God," I say. But I don't say more. The irony is not acknowledged, if irony is what it is.

The restaurant is a franchise that exists in every

mall, in every city. Its windows look out onto the inside, a tiled floor, a planter and a fountain surrounded by benches on which people loll under skylights. Across the way is a Sunglass Hut, a Foot Locker, a Hallmark card shop—places so generic that they deny any notion of specific place and time. Looking at them, it's as if all the intervening life suddenly evaporates; I feel I could be anywhere at any time in the last twenty years, that I could be in the place I escaped. The sweat of fear gathers under my shirt and at the roots of my hair.

"We have to go," I say, standing suddenly, grabbing my satchel. "We'll miss our trains."

My half sister stands. "Okay," she says, and I see that she thinks the abrupt departure is odd but excuses it as proceeding from what she's always regarded as my high-strung nature.

On the train on the way home I become convinced that the invitation to meet her, the impassioned requests, are part of a plot. That she's been so nice and so forgiving because she's conspired with our father, and while I was eating the turkey sandwich that I throw up in the lavatory on the train, he has been murdering my husband and stealing my children.

What else might satisfy him but to destroy the life I've built despite him, to plunder another generation? What has he ever wanted but everything?

From the train's mobile phone I call and call my own number. No one answers, and I begin to sob, curled over on the seat before the telephone, my face in my lap.

"What's the matter?" a woman says. "Can I help you?"

I shake my head. I can't look up at her. Is there a way to tell a stranger that once upon a time I fell from grace, I was lost so deeply in a dark wood that I'm afraid I'll never be safe again?

When I get home, my family is fine. Husband, children. I weep with relief. I have to touch them all, I can't stop. Though they have never seen their grandfather, nor he them, my children pay, too, by having a mother who carries this darkness inside her. Even from afar, my father exacts a cost.

"What is it?" my husband says. "What happened?"

"Nothing," I say. "I tried to call. No one answered."

"Oh," he says. "I guess we were taking a walk."

We look at each other, my husband and I, a meaningful look, but we don't talk about my crying. In our marriage we've made a place for my father and what happened between me and him. It's a locked place, the psychic equivalent of a high cupboard, nearly out of reach.

My children touch my face, my hair. They kiss me. To them I am perfect and beautiful.

We're taught to expect unconditional love from our parents, but I think it is more the gift our children give us. It's they who love us helplessly, no matter what or who we are.

As if my father's house were some kind of punitive school—which, in a way, it is; I'll remember my time with him as filled with painful lessons—I spend holidays with my mother and her parents, all of whom are strangely kind to me, unprecedentedly gentle. As if by agreement, we never mention my father; we pretend that he doesn't exist. But we mourn for me, the lost child, the child snatched away by the lost father. We weep extravagantly at any opportunity: over fictive deaths on television, distant accidents in the newspaper. We cry over the tiny losses of flat tires, broken radios, spilled milk.

After Christmas, my mother and I shop together listlessly. We're going to the same party on New Year's Eve, one hosted by a friend of hers. She's buying me a dress to wear to that party; I'm to choose it with her from the overpriced Laura Ashley boutique. In the store, standing under her critical gaze, I am as I was as a child: I command my body to endure the process with as much dignity as possible, while I remain underground, contracted to an unassailable morsel deep within myself, too deep to exhume. It's not unlike the way I tolerate my father. This flesh, I tell myself, means nothing. You are not a body, but a heart, a mind, a soul. These are yours and no one can take them from you.

The dress costs a great deal and is something I will never wear again. It's made from beautiful fabric, a subtly luminous blue plaid, but I dislike its high neck and tight bodice, the long sleeves, wide sash, and white cotton petticoats meant to be worn so that they show several inches below the hem. With black patent-leather shoes and white lace tights, my blond hair falling whole feet past the bow in the back, I look like what my mother must wish I were: a chaste, pretty doll incapable of the sins I conceal.

After she buys my dress, she finds a low-cut one of black velvet for herself, and then we take the Galleria escalators back down to the garage.

"Here, let me carry your bags too," I say, holding

out my free arm. One tread below me, the wan winter sun falling onto her white face, my mother looks strangely frail. "Are you okay?" I ask.

"Tired," she says. "Just tired." But there's something in the droop of her shoulders, the way she lets her head fall forward, that frightens me. I don't think of the lump, cut out a year before. I don't think *cancer,* but I feel a visceral squirm of fear, my heart pounds erratically. In the future, when I remember my mother, I'll recognize that instant on the moving stairs as the point at which I begin to understand that I will lose her. The pallor of her face, its ghostly translucence, predicts that what I've always feared will come to pass; it whispers that the woman I have pursued for all my life will vanish.

When we dress for the party, my mother tells me what makeup to wear, and I obey. "Put on some rouge," she says. "Promise me, if you don't have a tan, you'll always wear rouge."

"All right," I say.

The party is comprised of people I have never met, all of us gathered in a beautiful glass house on a hill overlooking the city. My mother's companion is with us. He drinks too much and we don't drink at all, as is usual when the three of us are together. We sit before a strange late meal of potatoes and bratwurst and various pâtés, slices of rare meat bleeding on the white china. Our Austrian hostess calls us to attention by striking a spoon against her champagne glass. She announces that in the town where she was born it's considered inauspicious to eat anything with fins or with wings on New Year's Eve, lest in the coming year your luck might swim or fly away.

My mother spears a coin of sausage from her plate. She holds it up on her fork as if in a toast. "So," she says, "I guess we're safe."

The clock strikes midnight, and my mother and I exchange a solemn kiss.

The next time I see my mother she's in the hospital, she and my grandfather both.

"What happened?" I say over tea at my grandparents' breakfast table.

"Oh," my grandmother says, "your mother's having tests and your grandfather's broken his leg, falling over the damn hose." She points through the kitchen window toward the pool, and when I go outside, I see by the coiled hose a yellow stain on the deck where he vomited from the shock of the break. I stare at the mark for a minute, perhaps longer, and then I go to get a scrub brush to remove what the paramedic's cursory rinsing did not.

My grandfather survives the surgery to repair his femur, his ninety-three-year-old bone pinned together with four long stainless-steel nails, but then he gets gangrene from a bedsore on his heel, and the painstakingly reassembled limb is amputated. He survives that surgery as well, a strong heart cursing him to a few more months in hospitals and nursing homes, where first the lining of his stomach and then his gall bladder and then everything else gives out.

CAT scans reveal that my mother's back is hurting her because it's broken. Her vertebrae are beginning to crumble because of metastatic breast disease. X rays show that her cough won't go away because her lungs are riddled with cancer, as is her liver. The blood-gas profile says she's tired all the time because she's not getting enough oxygen.

• • •

They both die slowly, and as they do I return to them, and to my grandmother.

I fall into a pattern of spending two weeks at my father's house and then two weeks at my grandparents'—that amount of time representing the limit of my ability to bear either place and its pain. At my grandparents' house, my grandmother and I sleep in the same room, I in my grandfather's twin bed pushed up next to hers. We keep the telephone between our two pillows in case one of the hospitals calls during the night; and I realize, lying awake beside her in the dark, that this is the closest I've felt to anyone in years.

Each day at teatime we visit my grandfather. We bring him his tea in a thermos, along with two cookies in a Baggie. My grandmother has had tea with my grandfather every day for more than forty years, and she will do so until the last day of his life.

We see my mother after dinner, and in her room we watch television on the set bolted to the wall over our heads. We watch nighttime soaps like *Dallas* or *Dynasty*, shows in which people often scream or sob, and my mother and I cry with them. My grandmother doesn't cry while she's awake, but one night I listen as she cries in her sleep. It's an odd noise, a little *uh-uh-*

uh, like the sound puppies or babies make while nuzzling at their mothers for a nipple. But it's definitely crying. Her face is wet, tears leak from under her closed eyelids, and sometimes she interrupts herself to speak.

"Oh, no, no, no," she says, still asleep, words I interpret as a prayer, so familiar an internal refrain are they.

"Does it mean I'm suicidal if I fantasize about my death, if I picture it?"

"How often?"

"Oh, you know, a couple times an hour anyway."

The doctor winces, rubs his eyes. When I tell him that my father and I have "this, uh, thing between us that is, uh, not platonic," he doesn't betray disgust or even disapproval, only weariness.

"Oh," he says, drawing a deep breath. "I see," he says, his sigh implying he's seen it before.

"It's not terrible?" I ask, after a silence.

"Aren't you shocked?" I say on another occasion. But he doesn't answer. He does not address moral questions, only those of feeling and function.

I've come to him because I'm afraid for my life. Because my father keeps a pistol in his house and he's taught me how to shoot it. So far, all I've done is load it; I've dropped the bullets into the chambers and clicked the cylinder in place. I've felt its weight in my hand, but then, ultimately, I've put both gun and bullets away in their separate drawers.

"Do you want to die?" the doctor asks.

I can't imagine remaining alive. I can't conceive of a life apart from my mother's. I know my grandfather's death will bring sorrow, but my mother's is too great and too impossible to even begin to consider.

"You did this to me!" she wails once, her tongue loosened by morphine. "You and your father are killing me!"

No! I think. *Us! Us!* Killing us. Not you. Never only you.

Sometimes, when she's afraid she'll die that very night, I spend it in the hospital with her. I sit in the chair by her bed or I stand beside her as I keep watch over her and over the little jet that delivers oxygen to the green tube that snakes up her nose. Once, she takes my hand. Eyes closed, she gropes for it, she calls my name. "Are you there?" she says.

"Yes," I say.

"You're always there, aren't you?" Her voice is not even as loud as a whisper. Like a ghost's, it's made of air.

"Yes," I say. Even when I'm with him, I'm standing by your bed. Especially then.

"Do you know," she says, "after I'm dead, you're going to be very angry with me." And then she says nothing else.

I squeeze her fingers, give them a little shake. I recognize the truth of her words without feeling them. Well, yes, I think, I guess you're right. But it will be a long time yet before I *feel* it. She'll have been dead for years before my anger cools enough to touch.

The doctor prescribes an antidepressant that I am to take each night before bed. I've told him I'm frightened by my own capacity for recklessness, for self-destruction. At my grandmother's house, hidden in the desk I used when I was a schoolgirl, are twelve Seconal capsules. They're old, their red gelatin sides stuck to one another. I began collecting them when I was fourteen. I pilfered one or two a month from the medicine cabinet. A dozen Seconal won't do much, though. I used to have forty, but I lost one, and once I tried it at midnight with twenty-seven and a tumbler full of scotch—all that I managed to swallow before I began throwing up. I never even passed out.

"You look a bit pale," my grandmother observed the next morning.

"I think I'm coming down with something," I said.

"What happened to your eye?"

"I don't know. I must have slept on it funny." My right eye was red on the inside corner from having broken a blood vessel while retching. Looking at her looking at me, I concluded that she had no idea of what had transpired in my bathroom only hours before.

When the doctor asks me if I want to die, I tell him I'm worried about myself, but I don't tell him about the sleeping pills because I'm too ashamed, a feeling I won't understand until years later, when what will strike me as more damning than my self-destructiveness is my capacity for secrecy, my genius at revealing so little of my heart—and thus the risk that I, too, could end up a woman as trapped within herself as my mother. I took the pills in the midst of an encompassing fog of despair, one I couldn't see beyond, not at all. Although it was as much as a year after my mother and I went to the gynecologist's office for a diaphragm, I connect the two events. I think I took them so that my body would die along with what else was murdered that day: girlhood, hope, any notion of being safe anywhere, with anyone.

The drug the doctor prescribes for me, Desyrel, paradoxically makes living both possible and, to the extent that I'm aware of it, unbearable.

"My life," I tell my father, "sucks. But I mean really, really sucks."

"Look," my father says. We're sitting at a picnic table at a roadside stop, the kind that truckers pull into for a few hours of sleep. "If it's the sex, we don't have to do it. It's just a means of expressing our commitment to each other. If it's not good for you, we'll find another way."

But what could serve both our needs so well as this compulsive, joyless coupling, the use of our bodies to express our desires? In this way we are not different from other people. My flesh, starved and lifeless under his, how eloquently it says what I cannot: I'm hungry, and I'm dead. Dead in allegiance to my mother, and dead to him as well. Dead in response to his using his big body to separate me from the world.

Trucks pass, one after another, and the wind they bring whips my long hair between our faces.

I don't want abstinence, I want release. "Please listen," I say. "What if one day I want to have a husband, children, a family like other people have? To be loved like other people are."

"What people?" he says.

"Other people. People who aren't like you or me." I look at him. "Normal people," I say.

"Who's normal? Normal is a mathematical concept. It has no bearing on human personality or relationships."

"You know what I mean! And you know I've tried. I've given you everything you've asked. I'm not saying that it's what you intended, but I feel so alone in the world. You won't let me have anyone, not anyone except you. And you have other people. You have a family."

"You can't expect me to leave my children," my father says.

"No, of course I don't. I don't want that at all. But what about me? I'm your child, too."

My father looks at me. "It's too late for you," he says.

"What are you saying?"

"I'm saying you've made a mistake." He leans forward. "We've talked about this, you know. How all the mistakes we make are permanent. How acts can't be undone."

"Yes," I say. "I know."

"Well," he says, and he folds his arms. "You've done what you've done, and you've done it with me. And now you'll never be able to have anyone else, because you won't be able to keep our secret. You'll tell whoever it is, and once he knows, he'll leave you."

I look at my father. I hear his words and, to the extent that I believe them, I hate him.

"This is irregular," the nurse says.

"I know," I say.

"We just don't do it." She walks quickly, in shifting

planes of white: white dress, white cardigan, white nylon tights, white shoes.

"Who do I have to see to get permission?"

"Wait here," she says, and she leaves me outside a glass-paneled office.

After making impassioned pleas to several hospital administrators and being passed from one cubicle to another, I finally secure admittance to the hospital morgue. The indulgence is granted because, as the paperwork attests, my grandfather's body will be taken directly from the morgue to the crematory, there will be no other opportunity for me to see it. "But," as the man who signs me in insists, "it's irregular, highly irregular."

My grandfather lies in his refrigerated drawer, his hands in fists under his chin, as if he found this position after he was brought to this cold room. His mouth is open, seemingly in protest against such chill.

I expect to be frightened by this corpse I have fought to see, but how can I be? The face and hands above the sheet are so familiar that what I feel is a rush of affection. The nurse leaves me with my grandfather, saying she'll be back after her break, and then I kneel beside him. I lay my head on his chest as I used to when I was small. I touch his eyebrows and his cheek, the white stubble of his beard.

His eyes are open and show me the same mild blue as they did in life; the pupils are clouded as if the cataracts, removed years before, have returned. I look at his eyes for a long time. How they amaze me, and teach me why it is the undertaker closes them.

Though I've courted and teased death, played irresponsibly with my life, I never believed in my own mortality until I sat beside my grandfather's cold body, touched and smelled and embraced it. All along, it was my unbelief that made recklessness possible. The hour I spend with my grandfather, kneeling by the long drawer, changes my life. The kiss I place on his unyielding cheek begins to wake me, just as my father's in the airport put me to sleep. I am transformed from a person who assumed she had time to squander to one who now knows that no matter how many years her fate holds, there will not be enough.

"Are you all right?" asks the nurse when she returns to the morgue and slides the drawer shut.

My hands are shaking with my new knowledge. I stare at her.

"I said are you all right?" she repeats.

"Oh," I say. "Yes."

At my grandfather's memorial service, the rabbi calls upon each of his descendants by name; he has us stand as he exhorts us to live our lives honorably. The service takes place just after Hanukkah, and the rabbi reminds us of lighting candles. He asks that we cherish the memory of my grandfather, who died during the feast of lights, that for him we go forth as brightly as possible and make our lives those of illumination, not darkness.

The words are sentimental, and they are spoken by a stranger, but they affect me. If the other mourners see how stricken I am as I contemplate the dishonor I bring to my grandfather's funeral, if they see the hot tears that come at the recognition of how dark my life has grown—well, undoubtedly they excuse those tears as proceeding from a grief more simple than mine can ever be.

"What are you doing?" my grandmother asks when she finds me a day later at the kitchen table, papers spread all over, searching through files I haven't opened in years.

"Applying to graduate schools," I say.

She looks at me. "Really?" she says. She sits down in the chair across from mine. "Where?" she asks, after a moment.

I name the cities where the schools are located, all far from my father's home. She nods. "Do you want tea?" she asks.

She fills the kettle. Neither of us articulates what is happening. That I am beginning to pick up the parts of my life that I dropped years before. We cannot say what we don't yet know: that what my grandfather's death has begun—my release—my mother's death will complete.

"Do you know," my father said in the car after we left the truck stop, "there's only one person who could have given you the strength to leave me."

And though we'd only driven a mile or so, he pulled over and stopped the car on the side of the road. He took off his glasses and leaned his forehead against the steering wheel. I looked at him.

"You?" I said, at last.

"Yes," he said.

When I was a small child, my mother would sit at her vanity table and brush my hair. The vanity table had opposing mirrors at its sides, and if I turned my head to the left or to the right I'd see the two of us multiplied endlessly, and I would read in that spatial infinity a message of temporal infinity as well: No matter which way I looked, back into the past or forward into the future, I would always see myself standing as obediently as possible under my mother's hands as they worked, the two of us united in the bond that would always define us, our trying to make me into the child she can admire and love.

Many of the nightmares I have about my mother concern hair. In the dreams, she cuts my hair off, she dyes it red or black, she locks me in a tower built of bathroom tile with walls too slick to scale. Like Rapunzel, my hair is so long that its length cannot be without meaning. I've always insisted on the excess of it to indicate the point at which I draw the line, to say that I would change only so much of myself to satisfy my mother.

For years my hair has been a symbol of *me,* of how I differ from my mother: long versus short, blonde versus brunette. I've absorbed myself in its care, cutting split ends out one by one with manicure scissors. The longer it gets, the more brushing it demands, especially since I won't braid or contain it with clips or elastics. "It's too long," my mother complains, and then I always have to grow it longer, there can't be enough of it to satisfy me.

My father is as dedicated to my hair as I am. For the past few years, he has been the one to trim it. Never trusting that anyone else would take the minimum amount, he has spent whole hours on his knees, using his scissors with absolute attention.

But during the last months of my mother's life I devote myself to her desires before my father's and before my own. She wants pink Kleenex, not white: I go out to get it. I bring food from distant restaurants, Vaseline in a tube, not a jar, French magazines, Swiss chocolate. Whatever whim she expresses I satisfy. We invent time-consuming errands for me to perform so that we are spared each other's company while I demonstrate my willingness to please her.

The stylist at the salon gathers my hair into an elastic and cuts, as I've asked him to, just above it. In the hospital, I lay the severed ponytail, twenty-three inches long, on her bed. She touches the hair.

"Well," she says, "it's about time."

Having my hair cut off and then giving it to my mother is a complex act, one with layers of meaning. There are things I need to tell my mother before she dies, before she leaves me; and I speak, as I always have, with the body she gave me, the one she carried inside her.

Within the haircut are, of course, love and anger: a hostile capitulation. I make my hair a sacrifice to my mother's vision of the daughter she wanted, a relic of the girl who lived to please her mother, and who will live no more because without her mother that girl can have no life. If I don't wait until my mother is dead to lay my hair in her casket, it's because I can't waste this last chance to secure her approval. To tell her how much I still want it—enough to at last give her the one part of me I've always held out of her reach.

"Turn around," she says to me as I stand at the foot of her bed and she pushes the little button that makes the head of the bed rise and lift her. "So," she says, when I'm facing her again. "There you are. All anyone's seen for years was hair." She gestures toward the tail. "Are you going to keep it?" she asks.

"What for?" I say, and she shrugs.

I end up throwing it out, letting it fall in a shining mass into one of the hospital garbage cans.

Long hair is an obvious symbol of sexuality, and for me it was the safeguard of my femaleness when I'd given up my breasts and my period. By cutting my hair off, I tell my mother that my sexual life is severed as well. Discarding it, I promise her that she can die knowing the affair between her husband and her daughter is finished.

How surprised I am, years later, when I see the altarpiece of the Church of Saint Dymphna in Gheel, Belgium. Sculpted by Jan van Wavre in the early sixteenth century, Dymphna's father cuts off her hair, a long blond tail of it, as much like my own as a statue's could be. Except that I don't let my father have that hair, or my life.

"Oh!" my father says when he sees me after the haircut. "My God," he says. "Dear God."

He grieves over the hair as he does not over my telling him I've been accepted in graduate school, that I'll be moving away in the next few months. "How could you take it from me!" he cries.

Malignancies in the bone are among the most painful of cancers, but they offer a solace that no other can. During the final weeks of my mother's life her bones deteriorate at such a rate that in places they almost dissolve, and as they do they release calcium into her bloodstream—enough calcium that the sedative property of the mineral is intensified to the point that she needs no morphine. The chemistry of her own death frees my mother from pain and anxiety, and each day she sleeps longer and more deeply, until at last she falls into a coma. Eyes closed, she no longer responds to the voices around her.

As I look at her, I remember that once, when I was five, I lifted her mask as she slept. Gently, without waking her, I pushed it up onto her forehead, and then, since I couldn't bear to look at her closed eyes—

to have her eyes perpetually closed to me—I tried to do the same with her eyelids. I pushed one up, very gently.

She woke in an instant, angry.

"I . . ." I whispered, stepping back. "I just wanted you."

"Don't ever do that!" she said. "Don't touch me!"

After that, she locked her door when she went to bed. For months she remembered to do it each night. But then one day she forgot. One morning when I tried the knob the door opened. And I returned to my place beside her, standing silently, not touching, just waiting. Waiting.

"Wait here," the undertaker says. "She'll be out in a jiffy."

When he returns, he's put his suit jacket on, as if the meeting between me and my mother's corpse requires a certain decorum. I follow him into the viewing room, decorated to look like a library with a wingbacked chair and bookshelves bearing, incredibly, a set of *Encyclopedia Britannica* bound in the same red leatherette as those my father sold my grandparents. Screwed into the fixture over the casket are pink light bulbs, like those my mother always used because she thought they made her look prettier.

I wait by the door until the undertaker leaves. I wait until I'm alone to go to her. She's small in the casket I chose. She lies so deep within it that I have to reach in to stroke her hair, rough and suddenly gray. Her cheeks are cool, dry, rouged. Her eyes are closed, and her lips as well. When I bend over her, I smell embalming fluid.

I touch her chest, her arms, her neck; I kiss her forehead and her fingertips; I lay my warm cheek against her cold one; and, as I do, something drops away from me: that slick, invisible, impenetrable wall. Whatever it was that separated me from my life, from the life I had before I met my father—the remains of what was built in an instant by his long-ago kiss—comes suddenly down. And as it does I gasp, I squeeze my mother's fingers. *Oh God, I'm sorry, I'm sorry,* I say. *My God, oh God, it's over.*

I reach under the bottom half of the lid for the catch to unlock it but find none. I slip my hand down as far as I can, past her knees, past the hem of her white dress. I want to touch and know all of her, want her feet in my palms.

Impossible to get my arms around her; she's too heavy to lift, her dress too slippery to allow me any purchase. I cry and my tears fall in her hair and on her face. Her hands come undone from the crucifix they held and fall to her sides.

I stay with my mother's body for an hour, longer. I stand by her casket until I grow tired, and then I pull up a chair so I can sit beside it. When I leave, I drive to my grandmother's home only to get back into the car and return to the mortuary. I ask the undertaker if he would please have my mother brought back to the viewing room.

"Again?" he says, sounding annoyed.

I nod. "Please," I say. Just once more I have to return to her side, touch her hair, her cheek. Just once more I have to make sure that it's true: the spell is broken, her death has released me.

At the funeral, serving as one of her pall bearers, my father knows, too, that it's over. He looks at me and sees that I am no longer his. He reads it in my eyes that return his gaze levelly, that suddenly don't find his eyes passionate or even mysterious, only bloodshot, weary. They narrow as he looks at me looking at him, and I see that he knows.

The realization, surprisingly, does not provoke tears, his or mine. Without my mother as witness, do I no longer bewitch him? It is one of the many questions I never ask my father, one that occurs to me only after our break from each other, abrupt and final: one phone call during which neither of us cries or begs or says the word *love.*

"It's all or nothing?" I ask. I don't want to be the one to say what I know is true: we can't start over, we have to say good-bye. Clumsily, I try to diffuse our agony with sarcasm. "You're not willing for the sake of novelty to try to be a little conventional? You know, the occasional phone call, birthday card?"

"Don't you know me yet?" my father says, his voice as low and as cold as I've ever heard it. "Don't you know my answer?"

"Yes," I say. "I know."

What else have the last years taught me if not that my father will take nothing less than all of me?

"Which do you choose?" he says after a long silence.

"Nothing," I say. "You know that I have to choose nothing."

His wife packs the things I left in his house, and my grandmother pays to have them shipped back to me. "Thank God," she says when I ask her for the money. She gives voice to the words still ringing in my head: "Thank heavens, it's over at last."

Having so long prayed for release—having begged fate for a deliverance I couldn't yet effect on my own—I don't expect our parting to be painful. But the loss of my father will grieve me; it will hurt and never cease hurting. I won't escape it any more than I escape my love for my mother or my remorse over how gravely I wronged her.

The loss of my father will haunt me as it did in the days long past, when I saw a man with no face walk the halls in our house. Somewhere in the world is a father I can't know. Once he was unknown in his absence, and now that I have known him, and he me, the rest of my life depends on our exile from each other.

. . .

After the graveside service, my father and I stand silently by my mother's casket, which is suspended over the dark, empty hole, awaiting descent. The plot my grandmother bought is a double-decker one, deep enough to leave room for her own remains to rest one day on top of my mother's.

But years later, when my grandmother dies, I disregard her wish to be buried in that grave. I have my grandmother's body cremated and I scatter the ashes myself. I won't leave her resting for eternity on top of my mother, won't leave my mother eternally under that weight.

When my mother's headstone comes, it bears only her name and the dates of her birth and death. As soon as I see it, I'm sorry that I didn't include the word *Beloved.*

On the day I ordered it, the day after she died, I sat beside my grandmother in the cemetery's business office and paged through the heavy book that illustrated the various styles of grave markers. I chose granite over bronze and I carefully picked among the types of lettering. But I left the space below the dates empty, because on that afternoon the only word that I could imagine carved in that blank struck me as one I didn't deserve to use, rather than the truth that it was. Is.

Beloved.

I don't keep a journal of my dreams, but on February 7, 1995, I have one so unusual that I mark the date on my calendar, writing the word *Mother.* For myself there's no need to record what happens in the dream. I know that I will always remember everything about it.

My mother finds me in my kitchen. It's early one winter morning, and I'm preparing breakfast for my family, still asleep upstairs. I'm startled when I look up from the cutting board and see her, and I'm frightened. The only dreams I ever have of my mother are nightmares. But she seems friendly, almost eager. The light that comes through the glass door and falls on her is absolutely clear and white: sun reflected by snow. She wears a tailored navy blue suit, cut with care from fabric so lovely and lustrous that it shines. I am surprised that she has come to me years after her death, and I am fascinated by every detail of her presence. Her lapels, even—how perfect they are! I want to touch them, *her,* but I am afraid of dispelling this ghost. I want to show her my children, but I can't risk leaving the kitchen to rouse them or scaring her away by calling out.

Yet she doesn't disappear, she is luminously real. With the split consciousness that sometimes characterizes a dream, I remark to my sleeping self that perhaps my mother's spirit is really with me, that I can't have fabricated a presence so convincing simply by virtue of longing.

"Oh Mother," I say at last, not daring to touch her, "you are so very beautiful, and you are wearing the most exquisite suit." She shrugs off the compliment as if she doesn't care how she looks, as if she is no longer concerned with such things, and I know that we are both thinking of how it was at the end, how cancer stole her youth and beauty, how it mocked vanity.

Nothing happens then, and yet everything transpires. My mother and I look closely at each other. We look into each other's eyes more deeply than we ever did in life, and for much longer. Our eyes don't move or blink, they are no more than a few inches apart. As we look, all that we have ever felt but have never said is manifest. Her youth and selfishness and misery, my youth and selfishness and misery. Our loneliness. The ways we betrayed each other.

In this dream, I feel that at last she knows me, and I her. I feel us stop hoping for a different daughter and a different mother.

Acknowledgments

I am indebted to Amanda Urban and Kate Medina for their continued faith and support, to Janet Gibbs for listening, to Dawn Drzal for reading, to Jill Simonsen for her friendship, and to Colin for everything.